W9-BNB-549

DATE DUE

AUG 1 0 2010	

BRODART, CO.   Cat. No. 23-221-003

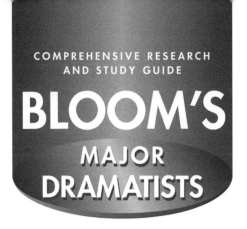

COMPREHENSIVE RESEARCH
AND STUDY GUIDE

BLOOM'S
MAJOR
DRAMATISTS

*Christopher
Marlowe*

EDITED AND WITH AN
INTRODUCTION BY HAROLD BLOOM

BLOOM'S MAJOR DRAMATISTS

Aeschylus

Anton Chekhov

Aristophanes

Berthold Brecht

Euripides

Henrik Ibsen

Ben Jonson

Christopher Marlowe

Arthur Miller

Eugene O'Neill

Shakespeare's Comedies

Shakespeare's Histories

Shakespeare's Romances

Shakespeare's Tragedies

George Bernard Shaw

Neil Simon

Sophocles

Tennessee Williams

August Wilson

BLOOM'S MAJOR NOVELISTS

Jane Austen

The Brontës

Willa Cather

Stephen Crane

Charles Dickens

Fyodor Dostoevsky

William Faulkner

F. Scott Fitzgerald

Thomas Hardy

Nathaniel Hawthorne

Ernest Hemingway

Henry James

James Joyce

D. H. Lawrence

Toni Morrison

John Steinbeck

Stendhal

Leo Tolstoy

Mark Twain

Alice Walker

Edith Wharton

Virginia Woolf

BLOOM'S MAJOR WORLD POETS

Geoffrey Chaucer

Emily Dickinson

John Donne

T. S. Eliot

Robert Frost

Langston Hughes

John Milton

Edgar Allan Poe

Shakespeare's Poems & Sonnets

Alfred, Lord Tennyson

Walt Whitman

William Wordsworth

BLOOM'S MAJOR SHORT STORY WRITERS

William Faulkner

F. Scott Fitzgerald

Ernest Hemingway

O. Henry

James Joyce

Herman Melville

Flannery O'Connor

Edgar Allan Poe

J. D. Salinger

John Steinbeck

Mark Twain

Eudora Welty

COMPREHENSIVE RESEARCH
AND STUDY GUIDE

BLOOM'S
MAJOR
DRAMATISTS

*Christopher
Marlowe*

EDITED AND WITH AN INTRODUCTION
BY HAROLD BLOOM

© 2002 by Chelsea House Publishers, a subsidiary of
Haights Cross Communications.

Introduction © 2002 by Harold Bloom.

Printed and bound in the United States of America.

First Printing
1 3 5 7 9 8 6 4 2

Library of Congress Cataloging-in-Publication Data
Christopher Marlowe / edited and with an introduction by Harold Bloom.
        p. cm. — (Bloom's major dramatists)
     Includes bibliographical references and index.
     ISBN 0-7910-6357-7 (alk. paper)
     1. Marlowe, Christopher, 1564–1593—Criticism and interpretation.
     I. Bloom, Harold.   II. Series.

     PR2673 .C46 2001
     822'.3—dc21   2001047544

Chelsea House Publishers
1974 Sproul Road, Suite 400
Broomall, PA 19008-0914

The Chelsea House World Wide Web address is
http://www.chelseahouse.com

Series Editor: Matt Uhler

Contributing Editor: Tara Mohr

Produced by Publisher's Services, Santa Barbara, California

Contents

User's Guide

This volume is designed to present biographical, critical, and bibliographical information on the author's best-known or most important works. Following Harold Bloom's editor's note and introduction is a detailed biography of the author, discussing major life events and important literary accomplishments. A plot summary of each play follows, tracing significant themes, patterns, and motifs in the work.

A selection of critical extracts, derived from previously published material from leading critics, analyzes aspects of each play. The extracts consist of statements from the author, if available, early reviews of the work, and later evaluations up to the present. A bibliography of the author's writings (including a complete list of all works written, cowritten, edited, and translated), a list of additional books and articles on the author and his or her work, and an index of themes and ideas in the author's writings conclude the volume.

~

Harold Bloom is Sterling Professor of the Humanities at Yale University and Henry W. and Albert A. Berg Professor of English at the New York University Graduate School. He is the author of over 20 books, including *Shelley's Mythmaking* (1959), *The Visionary Company* (1961), *Blake's Apocalypse* (1963), *Yeats* (1970), *A Map of Misreading* (1975), *Kabbalah and Criticism* (1975), *Agon: Toward a Theory of Revisionism* (1982), *The American Religion* (1992), *The Western Canon* (1994), and *Omens of Millennium: The Gnosis of Angels, Dreams, and Resurrection* (1996). *The Anxiety of Influence* (1973) sets forth Professor Bloom's provocative theory of the literary relationships between the great writers and their predecessors. His most recent books include *Shakespeare: The Invention of the Human*, a 1998 National Book Award finalist, and *How to Read and Why*, which was published in 2000.

Professor Bloom earned his Ph.D. from Yale University in 1955 and has served on the Yale faculty since then. He is a 1985 MacArthur Foundation Award recipient, served as the Charles Eliot Norton Professor of Poetry at Harvard University in 1987–88, and has received honorary degrees from the universities of Rome and Bologna. In 1999, Professor Bloom received the prestigious American Academy of Arts and Letters Gold Medal for Criticism.

Currently, Harold Bloom is the editor of numerous Chelsea House volumes of literary criticism, including the series BLOOM'S NOTES, BLOOM'S MAJOR DRAMATISTS, BLOOM'S MAJOR NOVELISTS, MAJOR LITERARY CHARACTERS, MODERN CRITICAL VIEWS, MODERN CRITICAL INTERPRETATIONS, and WOMEN WRITERS OF ENGLISH AND THEIR WORKS.

Editor's Note

My Introduction ponders aspects of the influence of Christopher Marlowe upon William Shakespeare, and attempts a brief estimate of Marlowe's dramatic poetry.

Marlowe's five major plays are examined here in critical extracts from twenty-one exemplary commentators.

Una Ellis-Fermor traces the change in Marlowe's Tamburlaine, from a visionary poet to a half-crazed tyrant, while A. C. Bradley commends the dramatist's achievement, given his short life. The great Australian poet A. D. Hope brilliantly captures Tamburlaine's "argument of arms," after which the scholar Kimberly Benston accurately describes the poet-tyrant's rhetoric as a contest of will, and Matthew Proser sees that contest as destruction, cultivated as an art.

George Wilson Knight, a major critic now too little appreciated, explores the relationship of aesthetic idealism and sexual sadism in the *Tamburlaine* plays. For D. J. Palmer, *Tamburlaine* progresses from a force of nature to a will overturning nature, while Muriel Bradbrook also detects a sadistic element reigning over Part II.

Dame Helen Gardner discusses limitations of the hero's will in Part II, after which C. L. Barber reads Tamburlaine's lament for Zenocrate as relying upon a neo-Christian imagery, one that Marlowe had sought at least to evade.

Marlowe's masterpiece is the tragic farce, *The Jew of Malta*, whose hero-villain Barabas is seen by Ellis-Fermor as bold and astute, while Harry Levin finds Machiavelli's "policy" to be dominant, and Douglas Cole wishes to see the protagonist as a symbolic rather than naturalistic being.

Wilbur Sanders shrewdly notes Marlowe's equal disdain for Christians and Jews, after which Clifford Leech examines the different strains of comedy in *The Jew of Malta*.

The great English Romantic critic William Hazlitt judges *Doctor Faustus* to be Marlowe's finest work, while Harry Levin clarifies the relationship between Faustus and Mephistopheles, seeing in the devil a sympathetic understanding of the aspiring magus.

Wilson Knight returns with a reflection upon Marlowe's limitations in *Doctor Faustus,* after which the still-lamented Angelo

Bartlett Giamatti sees the play's sub-plot as a deliberate trivialization of the plot. Marlovian limitation is considered also by C. L. Barber, while A. D. Nuttall, an admirable critic, introduces a Calvinism contaminated by Gnosticism into our estimate of the fate of Faustus.

Hazlitt notes the overall dramatic inadequacies of *Edward II*, but grants the poignance of the monarch's death. Swinburne, now under-esteemed both as poet and as critic, also praises the death-scene, and notes Marlowe's effect upon Shakespeare. While Ellis-Fermor judges Edward to be a charming degenerate, Charles G. Masinton emphasizes the king's suffering, and Irving Ribner finds in it an authentic approach to tragedy on Marlowe's part.

Introduction

HAROLD BLOOM

Christopher Marlowe, eliminated with maximum prejudice by Walsingham's Elizabethan Secret Service, was an astonishing dramatic poet, but possessed more insight into rhetoric than into human nature. Persuasive as Marlowe's language was, his characters are deliberate cartoons, parodied by Shakespeare in the farcical slaughterhouse of *Titus Andronicus*. Yet Marlowe, himself a wild original, was Shakespeare's starting-point, curiously difficult for the young Shakespeare to exorcise completely. We can surmise that Shakespeare sat in the theater in 1587, awed by the effect of the two parts of *Tamburlaine the Great* upon the audience.

Marlowe's accents can be detected in Shakespeare's three-part *Henry VI* and its sequel, *Richard III*, but not in Shakespeare's early comedies, or elsewhere in Shakespeare after 1594, except mockingly or otherwise deliberately. And yet that means the strongest writer known to us served a seven-year apprenticeship to Christopher Marlowe, only a few months older than himself, but London's dominant dramatist from 1587 to 1593, the year of Marlowe's extinction by the authorities.

The Marlovian protagonists—Tamburlaine, Barabas, Faustus, Edward II, the Guise in *The Massacre at Paris*—are all hero-villains, imitated by Shakespeare's Richard III and reduced to farce by his Aaron the Moor in *Titus Andronicus*. Iago, and the Edmund of *King Lear,* and Macbeth almost infinitely transcend Marlowe's eloquent caricatures, though it is fascinating to observe that Barabas in particular is their ultimate origin.

Barabas charms and delights me, as Shakespeare's Jew cannot, and Shylock, enigmatic and profound, is another huge instance of the overgoing of Marlowe by his early imitator. Because of Shakespeare's enormous influence upon all of us, it is very difficult now to revive the impression Marlowe first made upon his contemporaries. What was it like hearing the actor Alleyn "threatening the world with high astounding terms"?

In Act I, Scene 2 of *Tamburlaine, Part One,* the king of Persia sends a thousand horsemen led by the gallant Theridamas against Tamburlaine and his five hundred foot-brigands. Before battle commences, Tamburlaine addresses the Persians:

If thou wilt stay with me, renowmed man,
And lead thy thousand horse with my conduct,
Besides thy share of this Egyptian prize,
Those thousand horse shall sweat with martial spoil
Of conquer'd kingdoms and of cities sack'd.
Both we will walk upon the lofty cliffs;
And Christian merchants, that with Russian stems
Plough up huge furrows in the Caspian Sea,
Shall vail to us as lords of all the lake.
Both we will reign as consuls of the earth,
And mighty kings shall be our senators.
Jove sometimes masked in a shepherd's weed,
And by those steps that he hath scal'd the heavens
May we become immortal like the gods.
Join with me now in this my mean estate,
(I call it mean, because, being yet obscure,
The nations far-remov'd admire me not,)
And when my name and honour shall be spread
As far as Boreas claps his brazen wings,
Or fair Boötes sends his cheerful light,
Then shalt thou be competitor with me,
And sit with Tamburlaine in all his majesty.

This invitation is made to the audience; it is we who are to share in a glory that will subdue the kings of the earth, and Theridamas speaks for us when he yields to Tamburlaine's "persuasions . . . pathetical." Theridamas utters the rhetorical question: "What strong enchantments tice my yielding soul?", and we too are enticed. In 1587, the triumphal marches of Tamburlaine's rhetoric encountered no defences:

And ride in triumph through Persepolis!—
Is it not brave to be a king, Techelles!
Usumcasane and Theridamas,
Is it not passing brave to be a king,
And ride in triumph through Persepolis?

Shakespeare's defence against this verbal intoxication resolved at last into the figure of Ancient Pistol, follower of Sir John Falstaff, who himself mocks Pistol's fustian rant. Tamburlaine projects not only Marlowe's subversive spirit-gnostic, bisexual, counterspy, street-brawl-knifer—but also the poet's dizzy alternation of sadistic frenzy and Ovidian exaltation of Eros. When Damascus sends forth its fair young virgins to plead for the city, Tamburlaine commands that they be impaled upon his horsemen's spears, and then immediately chants a paean to his beloved Zenocrate:

> What is beauty, saith my sufferings, then?
> If all the pens that ever poets held
> Had fed the feeling of their masters' thoughts,
> And every sweetness that inspir'd their hearts,
> Their minds, and muses on admired themes;
> If all the heavenly quintessence they still
> From their immortal flowers of poesy,
> Wherein, as in a mirror, we perceive
> The highest reaches of a human wit;
> If these had made one poem's period,
> And all combin'd in beauty's worthiness,
> Yet should there hover in their restless heads
> One thought, one grace, one wonder, at the least,
> Which into words no virtue can digest.
> But how unseemly is it for my sex,
> My discipline of arms and chivalry,
> My nature, and the terror of my name,
> To harbour thoughts effeminate and faint!
> Save only that in beauty's just applause,
> With whose instinct the soul of man is touched,
> And every warrior that is rapt with love
> Of fame, of valour, and of victory,
> Must needs have beauty beat on his conceits.

Marlowe plays to the audience's sado-masochism, then as now, and to its fondness for erotic sugar-plums scattered among the perverse *frissons*. By the time we reach Act IV of Part Two, the Marlovian rhetorical frenzy achieves an unhealthy ecstasy:

> Now crouch, ye kings of greatest Asia,
> And tremble when ye hear this scourge will come
> That whips down cities and controlleth crowns,
> Adding their wealth and treasure to my store.
> The Euxine sea, north to Natolia;

The Terrene, west; the Caspian, north north-east;
And on the south, sinus Arabicus;
Shall all be loaded with the martial spoils
We will convey with us to Persia.
Then shall my native city Samarcanda,
And crystal waves of fresh Jaertis' stream,
The pride and beauty of her princely seat,
Be famous through the furthest continents.
For there my palace royal shall be plac'd,
Whose shining turrets shall dismay the heavens,
And cast the fame of Ilion's tower to hell.
Thorough the streets, with troops of conquer'd kings,
And in my helm a triple plume shall spring,
Spangled with diamonds, dancing in the air,
To note me emperor of the three-fold world;
Like to an almond tree y-mounted high
Upon the lofty and celestial mount
Of ever-green Selinus, quaintly deck'd
With blooms more white than Herycina's brows,
Whose tender blossoms tremble every one
At every little breath that thorow heaven is blown.
Then in my coach, like Saturn's royal son
Mounted his shining chariot gilt with fire,
And drawn with princely eagles through the path
Pav'd with bright crystal and enchas'd with stars
When all the gods stand gazing at his pomp,
So will I ride through Samarcanda streets,
Until my soul, dissever'd from this flesh,
Shall mount the milk-white way, and meet him there.
To Babylon, my lords, to Babylon!

This is glorious, and aesthetically a dead-end. It is delicious, but I prefer its parody in Ancient Pistol. Tamburlaine is a poetry-machine; Marlowe winds him up, and he spouts forth again, but he is a personage rather than a person. The sly Barabas is also a monster, rather than a representation of the human, but he is endowed with a savage wit. I delight in his boasting speech to his Moorish henchman, Ithamore:

As for myself, I walk abroad a-nights,
And kill sick people groaning under walls.
Sometimes I go about and poison wells;
And now and then, to cherish Christian thieves,
I am content to lose some of my crowns,

That I may, walking in my gallery,
See 'em go pinion'd along by my door,
Being young, I studied physic, and began
To practise first upon the Italian;
There I enrich'd the priests with burials,
And always kept the sexton's arms in ure
With digging graves and ringing dead men's knells.
And, after that, was I an engineer,
And in the wars 'twixt France and Germany,
Under the pretence of helping Charles the Fifth,
Slew friends and enemy with my stratagems:
Then after that was I an usurer,
And with extorting, cozening, forfeiting,
And tricks belonging unto brokery,
I fill'd the gaols with bankrupts in a year,
And with young orphans planted hospitals;
And every moon made some or other mad,
And now and then one hang himself for grief,
Pinning upon his breast a long great scroll
How I with interest tormented him.
But mark how I am blest for plaguing them:
I have as much coin as will buy the town.
But tell me now, how hast thou spent thy time?

You can measure the distance from Marlowe to Shakespeare by wickedly interchanging lines between Barabas and Shylock. Think of Shylock gliding upon stage to proclaim: "Sometimes I go about and poison wells," while Barabas would come on to question: "If you prick us, do we not bleed?" Marlowe was a gorgeous overture, but the music of humanity arrived with Shakespeare. ❁

Biography of
Christopher Marlowe

Christopher Marlowe was born in Canterbury in 1564, the same year of Shakespeare's birth. He was twenty-nine years old when he died. Had Shakespeare's life ended at the age of twenty-nine, only his earliest works would have been passed down to us. Contemplating what Marlowe produced in his short career, one is compelled to wonder what works were left unwritten by this gifted poet whose literary development was cut short.

Scholars continue to wonder, as they have for over four hundred years, about the circumstances and cause of Marlowe's murder in 1593. The basic facts of his early life are clear: Marlowe was the son of a shoemaker and his troubled family had several quarrels with the law. Marlowe benefited from scholarships throughout his schooling, and attended the King's School in Canterbury, going on to Corpus Christi College, Cambridge. He attended Cambridge with the assistance of a scholarship associated with the Archbishop Matthew Parker, given to students intending to take Holy Orders. He received his B.A. in 1584 and continued to study for his master's degree. His university attendance became increasingly sporadic and his lengthy absences led the university officials to threaten to withhold his degree. Marlowe must have stunned the administrators when he presented a letter from the Queen's Privy Council, which explained these absences with the opaque but suspicious statement that Marlowe "had done Her Majestie good service, and deserved to be rewarded for his faithfull dealinge."

This incident has led scholars to speculate that Marlowe was involved in important and covert government activities that were related to his murder several years later. Based on the available evidence, it does not seem unreasonable to conclude that Marlowe was working abroad as a spy during his college years, possibly in Rheims among the Jesuits. There is considerable information suggesting that Marlowe continued his clandestine activities after he left Cambridge for London in 1587, where he worked as a playwright. Scholars share some consensus that around this time, Marlowe composed *Dido Queen of Carthage,* and worked on his translations of Ovid and Lucan, but the chronology of Marlowe's work continues to be a subject of much debate. It is known, however, that both parts of *Tamburlaine* were produced in 1587. *Tamburlaine* and Marlowe's other plays all enjoyed great popular success, though only *Tamburlaine* was published during his lifetime.

We have little information about Marlowe's personal life during his years in London. He and the playwright Thomas Kyd shared a room in 1591, and Marlowe most likely was part of a group of young intellectuals in London that included Sir Walter Raleigh. Marlowe's reputation among critics and readers as a daring and somewhat unruly personality is in part based on his bouts with the law: Marlowe was arrested in 1589 for being present at a murder and in 1592, he was arrested for counterfeiting in Flushing, known to be a center of spy activity. In a different incident that year, he was bound over to keep the peace.

The inquest report of Marlowe's murder on 30 May, 1593 explains that Marlowe had spent the day with three gentlemen, walking and talking with them in the garden. In the evening, the men went to a Deptford tavern where they quarreled over the bill. As the argument escalated, Marlowe drew his dagger, and wounded his companion Ingram Frizar who, in self-defense, stabbed Marlowe over his right eye, killing him.

There is much information suggesting that this account is a cover for a calculated murder. Ingram Frizar was employed by Sir Thomas Walsingham, cousin to Francis Walsingham, head of the Queen's intelligence service. Frizar was swiftly pardoned for the murder. Three weeks prior to his murder, Thomas Kyd was arrested for possession of heretical papers which he confessed belonged to Marlowe. Kyd, imprisoned and subject to torture, made accusations against him. Two days after Marlowe's death, Richard Baines gave authorities a written list documenting Marlowe's blasphemy and atheism, demanding that the dangerous man must be stopped.

Marlowe's death remains shrouded in mystery, and as Peter J. Smith remarks, "Nothing in Marlowe's life immortalized him like the leaving of it." Critic A. C. Bradley astutely reflects upon the ways in which Marlowe's early, unnatural death has shaped critical perception of him:

> Marlowe has one claim on our affection which everyone is
> ready to acknowledge: he died young. We think of him

along with Chatterton and Burns, with Byron, Shelley and Keats. And this is a fact of some importance for the estimate of his life and genius. His poetical career lasted only six or seven years, and he did not outlive his 'hot days, when the mad blood's stirring.'

The notion of Marlowe as a young playwright, whose "mad blood" helped to create his dramas, led many critics to associate Marlowe with his protagonists. They often surmised that the villain Barabas, the brutal Tamburlaine, the scholar Faustus, who like Marlowe, was learned in theology, were each surrogates for the playwright, representations of aspects of his personality or projections of his desires. Professor J. B. Steane eloquently describes Marlowe as so many early twentieth century scholars imagined him:

> There was a time not so very long ago when literary gentlemen could meet, say 'Christopher Marlowe' to each other, and be fairly sure that they were going to talk about the same person. . . . Thirty years ago Christopher Marlowe was a colorful character certainly, but a relatively simple one, all black and red: a rebel, an atheist, a fiery soul whose works expressed his own heady exuberance, aspirations and despairs. . . .

Yet, scholarly estimation of Christopher Marlowe as a personality has dramatically evolved. The simple conception of his atheism has developed into an appreciation for Marlowe as a poet who dealt subtly and ironically with the tensions between the secular and religious values of his day, complexly exploring the relation between human and divine and challenging the paradoxes and hypocrisies of theology and religious institutions. The identification of Marlowe with his protagonists has given way to the understanding of a more dynamic relationship between Marlowe and his creations. As Steane writes, from the perspective of modern scholars, he is regarded as "a writer deeply concerned with suffering and evil, morality and religion; an ironist and a detached observer." ❀

Plot Summary of
Tamburlaine the Great I

Tamburlaine Part I opens as Mycetes, King of Persia, laments to his brother, "Brother Cosroe, I find myself agriev'd; / Yet insufficient to express the same, / For it requires a great and thundering speech" (I.i.1–3). The inarticulate King, who can neither summon bold words nor express his emotions, is soon revealed to be a dim-witted coward swiftly overcome by Tamburlaine. Mycetes' defeat sets the stage for the rest of the action, and guides the reader to the essence of Tamburlaine's power, his own "great and thundering speech" (I.i.3). Tamburlaine's conquests are never directly presented to the readers, but his astonishing poetry, which is Marlowe's primary interest and focus, constitutes the Scythian's true strength and brilliancy. Sadism, ambition, and martial conquest are the most patent themes of the play, but underlying the action of the drama persists a deep exploration of the effects of potent words.

Mycetes, aided by generous counsel from his advisors, sends Theridamas and an army to kill Tamburlaine, "the Scythian thief" (I.i.36), who, "daily commits incivil outrages" (I.i.40) and aspires to rule Asia. Cosroe, brother to Mycetes, bemoans the decline of the empire under Mycetes' rule, describing the King's soft and fickle disposition thus laying the foundations for a dramatic contrast to the temperament of Tamburlaine. In the hope that Cosroe will recover the glory of the empire, several noblemen crown him Emperor of Asia and Persia.

In **the next scene,** the reader is introduced to Tamburlaine, who has kidnapped Zenocrate, daughter of the Soldan of Egypt. She entreats him to release her, but Tamburlaine explains that her "fair face and heavenly hue / Must grace his bed that conquers Asia" (I.ii.36–37). He then proudly describes, with utter certainty, his future as a mighty conqueror, "which gracious stars have promis'd at [his] birth" (I.ii.92). Zenocrate courageously protests against his cruelty to the innocent, and Tamburlaine replies by declaring his love for Zenocrate, vividly describing the luxuries and honors she will enjoy at his side.

As Theridamas and the soldiers approach, Tamburlaine's advisors are eager to charge into battle, but Tamburlaine, revealing himself to be a shrewd strategist, chooses to first speak with Theridamas. He works a brilliant seduction of wit and flattery upon Theridamas, again describing his future empire and promising Theridamas positions of power and honor. Theridamas, stunned at his own traitorous act, is persuaded by his words and joins in support of Tamburlaine.

Act II presents Tamburlaine's first major victories, which further portray his supreme confidence in battle and his rapacious ambition. As Menaphon describes Tamburlaine's imposing appearance, Cosroe wisely recognizes that Tamburlaine is destined to be "famous in accomplished worth" and plans to enlist the Scythian's support in the fight against Mycetes. Furious that he has been betrayed by Theridamas and Cosroe, Mycetes declares that he will kill Tamburlaine and his brother.

Just as he seduced Theridamas by his persuasive poetry, Tamburlaine thrills Cosroe with promises of the wealth and power they will win together. His rhetoric is effective and Cosroe replies, "Thy words assure me of kind success" (II.iii.61). They depart to charge Mycetes' approaching army.

In **Act II, Scene iii**, one of the most comical episodes of the drama, an overconfident Mycetes delights in his "goodly stratagem" (II.iv.11)—hiding the crown that Tamburlaine's army covets. Tamburlaine discovers him and teases the king for his cowardly act, snatching the crown from him, and returning it with a promise to take it back again in armed conflict.

Victorious after the battle, Cosroe crowns Tamburlaine regent and triumphantly orders the messengers to spread the news that "the Persian king is chang'd" (II.v.21). Moments after Cosroe departs, aspiring Tamburlaine turns to his followers and arouses their ambition by asking each if he would like to become a king. Tamburlaine then declares that he could attain the Persian crown and begins to prepare for a battle against Cosroe.

Scenes six and **seven** offer insightful considerations of Tamburlaine. Baffled by Tamburlaine's "giantly presumption" (II.vi.2), Cosroe and his men attempt to understand the conqueror. Meander surmises, "Some powers divine, or else infernal, mix'd / Their angry seeds at his conception" (II.vi.9–10). Ortygius questions, "What god, or fiend, or spirit of the earth" (II.vi.15) Tamburlaine might be. After the battle, a wounded Cosroe stands before Tamburlaine decrying his treachery. In one of the key passages of the play, Tamburlaine offers a justification of his ambition, explaining that the "thirst of reign" (II.vii.12) motivated him and arguing that nature teaches humans to have "aspiring minds" (II.vii.20). Cosroe dies and Tamburlaine is crowned Emperor of Persia.

In the opening of **Act III**, famed Bajazeth, Emperor of the Turks sends a messenger to inform Tamburlaine that if the Scythian consents to stay out of Africa and Graecia, he will keep a truce with him.

In **Scene two**, forlorn Zenocrate confesses to the Median Lord Agydas that Tamburlaine's "exceeding favours" (III.ii.10) handsome countenance, and poetic words have altered her initial distain for her captor and she now adores him. Tamburlaine overhears Agydas expressing his disapproval of Zenocrate's affection. Upon seeing Tamburlaine, Agydas astutely concludes that Tamburlaine intends to viciously murder him, and therefore stabs himself.

Tamburlaine scoffs at Bajazeth's messenger's admonitions and proudly affirms that he will defeat the Emperor's army. Act III then becomes an impressive battle of words. It is this competition of rhetoric, and not the fight on the field, that Marlowe directly portrays to readers. Tamburlaine and his men verbally inspire themselves for the battle, asserting that victory is sure. Tamburlaine underscores the important of this speech, responding to Theridamas' boasts with, "Well said, Theridamas! Speak in that mood, / For *will* and *shall* best fitteth Tamburlaine" (III.iii.40–41).

Tamburlaine offends Bajazeth with his casual address of the great Emperor, leading the two sides to exchange insults and provocations and Tamburlaine spits wonderfully witty retorts at Bajazeth and his contributory Kings. Bajazeth addresses an elaborate tribute to his Queen and Tamburlaine responds in kind, praising Zenocrate in exquisite poetry. As the warriors battle in the field, Zenocrate, Zabina and their maids, fight their own battle of words, sparring with increasingly vulgar descriptions of the base labors each will subject the other to when she prevails. Victorious, Tamburlaine revels in his triumph, and further infuriates the bound captives Zabina and Bajazeth by refusing to ransom them.

The Egyptian Soldan, father of Zenocrate, rouses his men to fight against Tamburlaine's nearby army.

Scene ii focuses on Tamburlaine's cruel degradation of Bajazeth, demonstrating a sadistic side of Tamburlaine's domination. He keeps Bajazeth in a cage and forces him to be his "footstool" (IV.ii.1). Bajazeth vehemently decries Tamburlaine and Zabina bewails the indignities her husband, once a revered leader, is made to suffer.

In Damascus, Tamburlaine pitches a white tent, a symbol of his offer of a temporary opportunity for peaceful surrender. If the city does not surrender, Tamburlaine's tent will be red, signifying the blood to be spilled in the siege. Zenocrate offers a plea that Tamburlaine have pity on her country and again suggesting Tamburlaine's commitment to his words, he replies, "Not for the world, Zenocrate, if I have sworn" (IV.ii.125).

Incensed by Tamburlaine's pride and barbarity, the Soldan and the King of Arabia agree to fight against Tamburlaine.

While banqueting during the siege on Damascus, Tamburlaine torments Bajazeth, who curses him, as words are the only available weapon of defense. Melancholy Zenocrate, grieving over her ravaged country, again asks Tamburlaine to raise the siege on Damascus. He refuses, but assures her that her father will be safe. They celebrate as Tamburlaine crowns his men kings.

In the **final act of the play**, Tamburlaine's tent is black, signifying his darkest moods of mercilessness. The desperate governor of Damascus sends Tamburlaine a group of virgins who he hopes "[w]ill melt his fury into some remorse" (V.i.22). The terrified virgins do their best to persuade Tamburlaine to pity the citizens, but he refuses to renege on his vow to destroy the city. Taking his brutality to an unprecedented height, Tamburlaine has the virgins slaughtered and hoisted up on the city walls.

Desperate Bajazeth and Zabina finally conclude that despite their curses, there is "no hope of end / to [their] infamous, monstrous slaveries" (V.ii.178). Bajazeth, losing his sanity from starvation and thirst, resolves to brain himself on his cage. When Zabina discovers her deceased husband she too brains herself. Upon finding them, Zenocrate, hysterical over her beloved's slaughter of her country, is seized by guilt and prays for pardon for Tamburlaine, and for herself, who, "was not moved with ruth / To see them live with so long in misery" (V.ii.308–9).

Tamburlaine and the Soldan prepare to fight each other, and Zenocrate is forced to choose her allegiance to her father or her love. She resolves to hope for Tamburlaine's "gentle" (V.ii.337) victory, with the life of her father being spared. Tamburlaine triumphs, and grants the Soldan the privilege of reign under Tamburlaine's greater rule. With the Soldan's approval, Tamburlaine, asserting that he has now won sufficient gains to rightfully honor her, crowns Zenocrate his queen and "takes truce with all the world" (V.ii.468). ❁

List of Characters in
Tamburlaine the Great I

Mycetes, the dim-witted King of Persia, is overthrown by his brother Cosroe with the help of Tamburlaine. While in power, Mycetes relies heavily on his advisor Meander.

Cosroe usurps his brother Mycetes and accepts a crown from the Persian nobleman and Medians who plotted to make him Emperor of Asia. He invites Tamburlaine to join with him and is shocked when Tamburlaine betrays him. Wounded in battle, he dies after cursing "[b]arbarous and bloody" (II.vii.1) Tamburlaine.

Meander wisely counsels Mycetes and takes over much of his responsibility as king. After the battle, Meander humbly accepts Cosroe's appointment as regent of Persia and lieutenant of his armies.

Theridamas, the Persian Lord, goes at Mycetes' bidding to kill Tamburlaine. He is quickly persuaded by the articulate Scythian to join with him. Later he helps to convince Cosroe to join in alliance with Tamburlaine.

Ortygius, follower of Cosroe, formally crowns him in Act I.

Menaphon is a Persian lord and supporter of Cosroe. In Act II, before Cosroe and Tamburlaine meet, Menaphon offers a vivid description of Tamburlaine's appearance to Cosroe.

Tamburlaine, the Scythian shepherd who aspires to rule Asia wins victory again and again throughout the drama, building his empire and subjecting his defeated enemies to his barbaric cruelty. Kidnapping and then wooing Zenocrate, Tamburlaine is a devoted and reverent companion for his beloved. A poet and tyrant whose words are themselves powerful weapons, Tamburlaine curses his enemies and inspires his followers with incredible language throughout the drama.

Techelles devotedly serves Tamburlaine, joins in the torment of Bajazeth and willingly carries out many of Tamburlaine's most brutal orders, such as the slaughtering of the virgins.

Usumcasane, a second loyal follower of Tamburlaine.

Bajazeth, Emperor of the Turks, is defeated by Tamburlaine and cruelly kept as his captive. Tamburlaine confines Bajazeth in a cage, and, in Act IV, makes him serve as a footstool. Bajazeth cries out to Mahomet, curses Tamburlaine, and admonishes him, "Tamburlaine, great in my overthrow, / Ambitious pride shall make thee fall as low" (IV.ii.76). Bajazeth repeatedly asks to die rather than be subject to more torture. Tamburlaine is unyielding and, after delivering an astonishing account of his desperation, Bajazeth commits suicide by braining himself on his cage.

King of Fez, King of Morocco, King of Argier the contributory kings of Bajazeth, who come to his support when Tamburlaine insults and offends him.

King of Arabia, betrothed to Zenocrate, agrees to fight with the Soldan against Tamburlaine. He returns from the battle wounded, and as he dies in Zenocrate's arms, tells her of her divine beauty and takes comfort in her presence.

Soldan of Egypt, father of Zenocrate, resolves to fight Tamburlaine with the help of the King of Arabia. Eager to win revenge for his daughter's abduction, he boldly cries out, "Now, Tamburlaine, the great mighty Soldan comes, / And leads with him the great Arabian king, / To dim thy baseness and obscurity, / Famous for nothing but theft and spoil" (IV.iii.63–66). Though he is defeated, the Soldan is pleased to learn that Tamburlaine has treated Zenocrate with honor, and offers his approval of their marriage at the close of the play.

Governor of Damascus realizes that his city will be destroyed and sends a group of virgins to plead with Tamburlaine for mercy.

Agydas speaks to Zenocrate about his love for Tamburlaine, but he urges her, to "[l]et not a man so vile and barbarous" (III.ii.26) be honored with her love. Tamburlaine and his men hear his words and soon Agydas suspects Tamburlaine's intention to kill him . . . hear his words and soon Agydas reads in Tamburlaine's expression his intent to kill him. To avoid being tortured and killed by Tamburlaine, he stabs himself.

Magnetes a Median lord, is captured by Tamburlaine with Zenocrate and Agydas.

Capolin is an Egyptian who shares his input and counsel with the Soldan and the King of Arabia as they plan to fight Tamburlaine.

Zenocrate, daughter to the Soldan of Egypt, is kidnapped by Tamburlaine. As his captive, Zenocrate first pleads with Tamburlaine to let her go, decrying his cruelty to the innocent and affirming that the Gods will never support his unjust tyranny. But, as she explains to Agydas in Act III, Tamburlaine wins her by his godlike appearance, graceful speech, and generous treatment toward her. In love with Tamburlaine, Zenocrate is not crowned his queen until the conclusion of the play, when Tamburlaine feels he has won sufficient honors to be worthy of her.

Anippe, maid to Zenocrate, joins in as Zenocrate and Zabina insult each other while Bajazeth and Tamburlaine fight.

Zabina, wife of Bajazeth is taken captive by Tamburlaine. She rails against the "[u]nworthy king that...[u]nlawfully usurp'st the Persian seat" (IV.ii.56–57). In Act V, her despair overtakes her and she cries out, "Then there is left no Mahomet, no God, / No fiend, no fortune, nor no hope of end / To our infamous, monstrous slaveries" (V.ii.176–178). She kills herself after discovering Bajazeth has taken his life.

Ebea, is maid to Zabina, and joins in Zabina's insults to Zenocrate as Bajazeth fights Tamburlaine.

Virgins of Damascus, reluctantly go, at the command of the Governor, to beg Tamburlaine for mercy. They are slaughtered and hung up on the city walls. ❀

Critical Views on
Tamburlaine the Great I

U. M. ELLIS-FERMOR ON THE EVOLUTION OF
TAMBURLINE'S CHARACTER

[Una Mary Ellis-Fermor was lecturer in English literature, Bedford College, University of London. She served as the General Editor of the New Arden Shakespeare and authored *Frontiers of Drama; Christopher Marlowe; Jacobean Drama: An Interpretation* and *Shakespeare the Dramatist*. In this excerpt she discusses the development of Tamburlaine's character throughout Part I of the play, and muses upon the transformation of his character in Part II.]

When the substance of Marlowe's story has been traced to its sources and his indebtedness therein acknowledged, all that remains is his own; the poetic conception that makes his play the only interpretation of genius that the life and aspiration of Tīmūr has ever received. ⟨. . .⟩

Tamburlaine embodies at first a poet's conception of the life of action, a glorious dream of quickened emotions, of exhilaration and stimulus that should 'strip the mind of the lethargy of custom', tear the veils from its eyes and lay bare before it in all-satisfying glory the arcana where the secret of life dwells, a secret ever elusive yet ever troubling men's desire. In happy exultation Marlowe fills with this figure the earlier scenes, unsuspicious of the crude, blunt passions that must necessarily be called up by blood and the intoxication of battle, of the wary vigilance, the practical alertness by which alone a rebel leader can preserve his life, the things that steal away the moment of vision and subdue the glowing colours of which 'youthful poets dream'. But as the first part of the play proceeds, his Tamburlaine changes. Marlowe himself perceives this strange conflict between the service of valour and the service of that beauty upon which valour yet depends. For a time a union between them is yet possible; the 'sum of glory' is 'that virtue' which can conceive and yet control the emotions stirred by beauty; the poet, exalted above the world of dreams and the world of actuality, holds both to their true task, shaping both to the service of supreme vision. In the second part of the play Tamburlaine changes still more; Marlowe had begun to perceive the discrepancy between his dream of the life of action and the world of practical life. The imaginative working out of his story had been enough to teach him this. There is little exultation or aspiration, only an overstrained repetition and exaggeration, a vigorous but futile effort to stimulate a tired imagination and to sweep again into the tireless, spontaneous rhythms of the earlier part.

But though the later figure fails of its earlier poetry, all is not lost. There is a gain in poignancy and in humanity. Tamburlaine, who breaks down into frenzy and half-insane rhetorical hyperbole, is humanly nearer to our understanding than the impenetrable, soaring visionary of the first part.

—U. M. Ellis Fermor, *Tamburlaine The Great* (New York: Gordian Press, 1930): pp. 52–54

A. C. BRADLEY ON THE DEVELOPMENT OF MARLOWE'S STYLE

[A. C. Bradley (1851–1935), renowned Shakespeare critic, is author of the classic work, *Shakespearean Tragedy*. In this excerpt Bradley discusses the development of Marlowe's style, comparing it with Shakespeare's and with conventions of the popular plays of the era.]

The two parts of 'Tamburlaine' are not great tragedies. They are full of mere horror and glare. Of the essence of drama, a sustained and developed action, there is as yet very little; and what action there is proceeds almost entirely from the rising passion of a single character. Nor in the conception of this character has Marlowe quite freed himself from the defect of the popular plays, in which, naturally enough, personified virtues and vices often took the place of men. Still, if there is a touch of this defect in 'Tamburlaine,' as in the 'Jew of Malta,' it is no more than a touch. The ruling passion is conceived with an intensity, and portrayed with a sweep of imagination unknown before; a requisite for the drama hardly less important than the faculty of construction is attained, and the way is opened for those creations which are lifted above the common and yet are living flesh and blood. It is the same with the language. For the buffoonery he partly displaced Marlowe substitutes a swelling diction, 'high astounding terms,' and some outrageous bombast, such as that which Shakespeare reproduced and put into the mouth of Pistol. But, laugh as we will, in this first of Marlowe's plays there is that incommunicable gift which means almost everything, *style;* a manner perfectly individual, and yet, at its best, free from eccentricity. The 'mighty line' of which Jonson spoke, and a pleasure, equal to Milton's, in resounding proper names, meet us in the very first scene; and in not a few passages passion, instead of vociferating, finds its natural expression, and we hear the fully-formed style, which in Marlowe's best writing is, to use his own words,

> Like his desire, lift upward and divine.

'Lift upward' Marlowe's style was at first, and so it remained. It degenerates into violence, but never into softness. If it falters, the cause is not doubt or languor, but haste and want of care. ⟨. . .⟩

The expression 'lift upward' applies also, in a sense, to most of the chief characters in the plays. Whatever else they may lack, they know nothing of half-heartedness or irresolution. A volcanic self-assertion, a complete absorption in some one desire, is their characteristic. That in creating such characters Marlowe was working in dark places, and that he develops them with all his energy, is certain. . . .

Marlowe had many of the makings of a great poet: a capacity for Titanic conceptions which might with time have become Olympian; an imaginative vision which was already intense and must have deepened and widened; the gift of style and of making words sing; and a time to live in such as no other generation of English poets has known. It is easy to reckon his failings. His range of perception into life and character was contracted: of comic power he shows hardly a trace, and it is incredible that he should have written the Jack Cade scene of 'Henry VI'; no humour or tenderness relieves his pathos; there is not any female character in his plays whom we remember with much interest; and it is not clear that he could have produced songs of the first order. But it is only Shakespeare who can do everything; and Shakespeare did not die at twenty-nine. That Marlowe must have stood nearer to him than any other dramatic poet of that time, or perhaps of any later time, is probably the verdict of nearly all students of the drama. His immediate successors knew well what was lost in him; and from the days of Peele, Jonson, Drayton, and Chapman, to our own, the poets have done more than common honour to his memory.

—Andrew Cecil Bradley, "The English Poets, Selections" ed. T. H. Ward (1880), I, 411–17, in *Marlowe: The Critical Heritage 1588–1896* ed. Millar MacLure (London: Routledge & Kegan Paul, 1979): pp. 127–128, 131.

A. D. Hope on the Humanism of War

[A. D. Hope, one of the major Australian poets of the twentieth century, served as Head of English at the Canberra University College. He became subsequently the foundation Professor of English at the Australian National University, retiring from this position in 1968. In this excerpt he explores the world view fueling Tamburlaine's actions, focusing on Tamburlaine's reply to Cosroe's angry reproach in Act II.]

The notion that knowledge is the highest of human aspirations is perhaps peculiarly a scholar's delusion and, in an age which worships knowledge, it is natural for scholars to misunderstand the passage in question. And this is especially so since kings have now fallen into such disrepute that to aspire to sovereignty over others has come to be regarded as a disgraceful if not actually a criminal ambition. But Marlowe's contemporaries would have no trouble in understanding Tamburlaine's drift, though they might not have understood the view of man and the world that underlies his argument. The humanism of this passage is in fact far removed from the humanism of the study or the laboratory. It is the humanism of war, a view in which all human values are determined by war alone.

What Tamburlaine says to Cosroe in effect is this: 'You think my conduct that of a barbarian and a greedy thief. On the contrary my action in making war upon my king and taking his crown was that of a god and made with the motive and the understanding of a god. For the gods may be assumed to know the nature of the world and they know that its principle is that of war. War is only incidentally destructive and disruptive. In essence it is the principle of order, the principle of beauty, and the principle of knowledge. The gods who established the world and their rule of it, did so by war. The whole state of Nature is one of perpetual strife. The elements of which our bodies are composed are in a state of constant strife and the order and growth of those bodies is the product of the strife. The same is true of the soul and its faculties, of the frame and structure of the world which the soul by its nature desires to comprehend, and of the social order in which each man has his place. That place is determined by strife and the highest human achievement is to become the master of men, the only being whose will is entirely free, the only being whose values are absolute in fact as well as in aspiration.'

The metaphysical conception on which the play is based is this theory of a universe in which order is the creation of strife and values are determined by strife. It is not a modern theory of 'might is right'; it is not a Nietzschean view of the will to power. It is based on the Aristotelian view that every creature strives towards the perfection of its nature. Man is the highest of the creatures and the perfection of his nature is to rule his world. Given the law of strife, the highest state of that perfection is to rule man himself. But those who actually rule usually do so, not by virtue of their absolute right to do so, for that right has not been tested by contest. This is where Tamburlaine differs from the hereditary kings. He has the natural genius for power and he actually tests it out against all possible contenders. He achieves the perfection of human nature in a world in which only one man can be perfect. This standard of values means that man who imposes his will on all others is, in a sense, the only fully human being among them.

—A. D. Hope, "'Tamburlaine': The Argument of Arms.'" In *Christopher Marlowe* (New York: Chelsea House, 1986): pp. 47–48

Kimberly Benston on Tamburlaine as Poet and Tyrant-Rhetor

[Kimberly Benston is the William R. Kenan Jr. Professor of English at Haverford College. He is a noted expert in the fields of African-American literature and Renaissance literature. In this excerpt he discusses Tamburlaine's engagement in a verbal competition of poetry and rhetoric that underlies the action of the play.]

For *Tamburlaine, Part One* (hereafter simply "*Tamburlaine*") as is clear from literally every line and scene, conflates verbal and physical power in the structure of rhetorical conflict which theorists from Longinus to Thomas Weiskel have termed the sublime. From his first appearance, Tamburlaine puts the ideological premises of rhetorical humanism to the dramatic test, literally making words into "woorking" instruments of desire while appropriately throwing off the limits of convention with the trappings of his "Parentage":

Lie here ye weedes that I disdane to weare,
This compleat armor, and this curtle-axe
Are adjuncts more beseeming *Tamburlaine*.
(237–39)

This, then, is the crucial import of Marlowe's revisionary insight into the immediate and secondary sources of Tamburlaine's character: in them Marlowe saw the fundamental lineaments of the antithetical temperament, however obscured by a contradictory metaphysical bias; and, concomitantly, he so shaped, intensified, and augmented them as to isolate the sublime crisis of violence and language for a dramatic examination of unprecedented vigor and complexity in English literature. In his resolute depiction of Tamburlaine as *tyrant-rhetor*, Marlowe evokes not the Ciceronian ideal of Tudor Humanists' ethical Orator King, but the sophistic wielder of violent *peitho*, the abrogator of law so feared by Plato for his realization of rhetoric as *tyrannikon ti*—a "soveraigne" mode of will.

From its inceptive invocation of Tamburlaine's engendering "high astounding tearms," the play emphasizes the conflictual aspect of rhetorical encounter from which the self emerges. The aura of excess and extremity suffusing such interchanges imbues Tamburlaine's claims upon divinity with significance beyond anything implied by liberal notions of "Renaissance individualism." At its most intense, the hero's linguistic assertion is also a defense against death and the primacy of Creation evoking the sublime's defining effort to appropriate the authority of origins. ⟨. . .⟩

Tamburlaine, in short, is structured in perfect accord with its philosophical and linguistic interests: it is a theatrical hyperbole, presenting the protagonist through an intensifying accumulation of conflicts (Tamburlaine's opponents, we recall, are increasingly formidable) which individually and collectively correlate heroism with violent, will-ful eloquence. The plot appropriately consists of a nearly unbroken chain of debates; as Donald Peet concluded, "there is scarcely a moment when one of the characters is not pursuing the primary goal of the rhetorician—persuasion." Form, like content, is here in a profound sense rhetorical. In saying this, we might seem to echo those who have found in Tudor rhetoric the embryonic model for Elizabethan drama and court with them the rejoiner that, as George Hunter has himself observed, the opposition of debate may be inherently dramatic but fine drama is more than argument. Effective theater, that is to say, must seek *movere* through dialectic and not simply dichotomy. This is precisely why it is crucial to understand Marlowe's rhetoric from a sophistic and sublime rather than a Humanist perspective: it is as a contest of *will* (*pathos*) and not of logic (*logos*) or attribute (*ethos*) that Marlovian heroism is enacted and realized. Rhetoric is thus not merely a vehicle of conflict but becomes, indeed, its essence; so that far from speaking in a uniform and monotonous manner *Tamburlaine*'s characters variously seek and achieve a heroic idiom articulated perfectly only by Tamburlaine. Marlowe's restriction of the figurative texture of his characters' speech to a few basic versions of 'amplification'—comparison, division, accumulation, etc.—is not the mark of poetic youth but of profound insight into the *agonistic* nature of hyperbole, the "outdoing" trope. Tamburlaine, we are to see, is first among rivals in a constantly escalating war for what Longinus called "the foremost place" in poetic competition.

—Kimberly Benston, "Beauty's Just Applause: Dramatic Form and the Tamburlanian Sublime." In *Christopher Marlowe* (New York: Chelsea House, 1986): pp. 208–209, 217–218

[Matthew N. Proser is Professor Emeritus in English at the University of Connecticut. He has published works on Shakespeare, Lawrence, Pirandello and Marlowe, and is the author of *The Gift of Fire: Aggression and the Plays of Christopher Marlowe*. In this article he offers a psychological analysis of Tamburlaine's passion for cruelty.]

This aspect of *Tamburlaine* seems worth considering: to what degree do destructive acts and words in fact shape the very form and being of Marlowe's play and in fact limit it? Suffice it to say that heroic conquest and its glories are a huge part of the manifest content of the drama. But if *Tamburlaine* is a dream "indulging . . . spellbound fancy in heroics," what is the precise relationship of "glory" to violence and cruelty in the play? Are these "realities" actually separable, or are they contained in one overridingly aggressive spirit that is communicated to the audience in such a way as to engender a shared response upon which we can all agree? If, as Levin offers, "destruction" is a "basis for creation" in the play, then what are the implications of this remark interpretively, and what does this insight reveal about Marlowe's creative process, and about his achievements and limitations in his *Tamburlaine*? ⟨. . .⟩

The repetitive pattern of Tamburlaine's career actually suggests that the goals of empery and adulation for acts of pure power are only part of the hero's purpose: that portion ostensibly meant to give him pride and pleasure. The other part is inflicting as much cruelty and destruction as he can, and with incrementing savagery. Tamburlaine must climb higher and higher because his passion to inflict pain outruns his achievements of status and power. And pain is where his true pleasure lies. Or to put the matter another way, the persistent ferocity of his aggression even after fulfillment hints that his real purpose is destruction not attainment. Achievement of "an earthly crown" or execution of "divine" wrath provide goals that legitimize a vengefulness which reacts dramatically to the inner accusation of "baseness" and all it could mean to Marlowe from his background relationship to his parents, his dead brothers, and his living sisters. This is the raw wound at the play's psychological center, the blind area of primary avoidance which incites astonishing deeds of military accomplishment so as to negate painful feelings of insufficiency by overlaying them with glory. Self-aggrandizement and glory serve as the vicarious pretext for the perpetual thirst to destroy in a kind of repetition compulsion. The "higher" aim, used to gild the "baser" one, finds its justification in the admiring eyes of those who worship "glory" for their own reasons. The need to strike back remains the primary defense both for Tamburlaine and his creator. In Tamburlaine, it takes the form of his destructively heroic behavior and its persistent repetitions in the play; in Marlowe it expresses itself in the very creation of his play. For Tamburlaine, any quiet moment might leave him open to the self-inflicted wound of self-doubt.

—Matthew N. Proser, "*Tamburlaine I* and the Art of Destruction" in *The Gift of Fire: Aggression and the Plays of Christopher Marlowe* (New York: Peter Lang, 1995): pp. 72, 84

Plot Summary of
Tamburlaine the Great II

Like Part I of the drama, Part II opens as a King discusses the threat of Tamburlaine. Yet Part II is markedly different from Part I in tone and focus. In Part II, Tamburlaine encounters the pacifism of his son, the death of Zenocrate, and finally, his own mortality. Each of these experiences challenges his mode of forceful conquest; he cannot conquer death, he cannot fight the heavens that have taken Zenocrate, and his demand for absolute domination leads him to brutally murder his own child. In Part II, Marlowe weaves a plot that implicitly challenges Tamburlaine's conduct and world-view to its limits.

Heeding his officer's counsel, King Orcanes decides to save his troops' strength for combat against Tamburlaine, and thus makes peace with the Christian King Sigismund of Hungary. The two kings seal their agreement as Sigismund vows to "[s]weet Jesus Christ" (I.ii.58), and Orcanes swears by "sacred Mahomet"(I.ii.60).

Like his father Bajazeth, Callapine endures a harsh imprisonment at Tamburlaine's hands. With a vivid description of the grand welcome that awaits him, Callapine persuades his keeper Almeda to help him escape, enticing Almeda with detailed accounts of the luxuries and rewards he will be granted. His skillful persuasion, won by words, recalls Tamburlaine's own potent poetry.

In **the following scene**, the reader finds Tamburlaine in a domestic milieu with Zenocrate and his sons. Marlowe's presentation of Tamburlaine in this smaller sphere and familial context marks a significant change from Part I of the drama. Zenocrate, weary of her husband's continual engagement in battle, dares to ask Tamburlaine when he will leave the dangers of war. Tamburlaine answers, "When heaven shall cease to move on both the poles, / And when the ground, whereon my soldiers march, Shall rise aloft and touch the horned moon" (I.iv.12–14). Tamburlaine shares with Zenocrate his worry that his sons seem "too dainty for the wars" (I.iv.28) but she assures him that they have "his conquering heart" (I.iv.36). As Tamburlaine praises Celebinus and Amyras for their martial spirit, Calyphas boldly asserts his desire to avoid the battlefield. Tamburlaine breaks out in a rage against him, roaring, "bastardly boy, sprung from some cowards loins / And not the issue of great Tamburlaine" (I.iv.69–70)! In **scenes five and six**, Theridamas, Usumcasane, and Techelles report to Tamburlaine on their troops and conquests.

In **Act II**, Marlowe returns to Sigismund and Orcanes, and through their plot line offers a fascinating consideration of the role of faith in war. Lords Baldwin and Frederick meet with Sigismund, and vehemently urge him to work revenge upon the "heathenish Turks and pagans," whom, they say, have cruelly slaughtered Christians throughout the region. Arguing that they have no obligation to keep their vows with such "infidels" (II.i.13) as Orcanes, and affirming that they have a religious obligation to scourge "foul blasphemous paganism" (II.i.6) and take advantage of Orcanes' divided army, they resolve to fight. When Orcanes learns of Sigismund's betrayal he questions the Christian faith, asking, "Can there be such deceit in Christians. . . . Whose shape is figure of the highest God" (II.ii.36,38)? In one of the most remarkable passages of the play, Orcanes takes the monumental step of praying to another's God. He appeals to Christ in an impassioned prayer for victory, believing that Christ, would "be reveng'd upon this traitors soul" (I.ii.58). After the battle, as Orcanes gives credit to Christ for his victory, wounded Sigismund cries out to God the "punisher of sin" (II.iii.4) whom he feels has afflicted him with a "well-deserved wound." (II.iii.6)

Gripped by anguish, Tamburlaine tends to an ailing Zenocrate, describing the cosmos darkening with her death, and imagining heaven's preparations to receive his beloved. As Tamburlaine rages against a force that he can neither battle nor rule, Zenocrate entreats him to let her die. When she passes, knowing no other way to respond, Tamburlaine orders his men to take up arms and "Batter the shining palace of the sun" (II.iv.105), and fight against Jove, who has taken Zenocrate from him. Only Theridamas dares to reply, humbly offering, "She is dead, / And all this raging cannot make her live" (II.iv.119–120). Tamburlaine has her interred until he dies, when they will share one tomb. Tamburlaine then burns the town where she died.

In **Act III**, Callapine, having successfully escaped, receives the imperial crown from Orcanes and the Kings of Trebizon, Soria, and Jerusalem. Rallying the kings for the battle against Tamburlaine, he passionately speaks of his father's suffering and affirms that inconstant Fortune will shift her allegiances and favor them in the fight.

Tamburlaine and his sons create several memorials to Zenocrate and the boys speak of their consuming sorrow. But Tamburlaine, as if unable to bear their indulgence in emotions, curtails this expression of grief and decides that he will teach them the "rudiments of war" (III.ii.54). When Calyphas shares his fear of being slain in this perilous martial training, enraged Tamburlaine cuts his own arm, and declares that "[a] wound is nothing. . . . Blood is god of war's rich livery" (III.iii.15–16).

At Balsera, Techelles and Theridamas threaten the Captain, who refuses to surrender. He is shot in battle and dies moments later, with his despairing wife Olympia at his side. Desiring that death carry her son's and her soul to her husband's, and fearing the torture that Tamburlaine's army will inflict, Olympia stabs her son and prepares to kill herself. Theridamas finds her and captivated by her beauty, ignores her pleas to be left in Balsera, declaring, "Madam, I am so far in love with you, / That you must go with us: no remedy" (III.iv.78–9).

Callapine and his kings prepare to fight Tamburlaine. As in Part I, Act III, the two sides wage a war of words. Tamburlaine outdoes his opponents in quick-witted descriptions of the horrible retribution he will subject them to after the battle. He boldly asserts that Heaven "never meant to make a conqueror / So famous as is mighty Tamburlaine" (III.v.83–84). Swearing to revenge his "father's vile abuses and (his) own" (III.v.91), Callapine incites Tamburlaine to the height of rage by crowning Almeda before his eyes.

In **Act IV**, Calyphas refuses to fight in battle. Throughout the play, Calyphas's rejection of his father's glorification of war serves as a powerful critique of Tamburlaine. Returning victorious, Tamburlaine rages at Calyphas and, ignoring the protests of Amyras, Theridamas, and Techelles, Tamburlaine stabs his son. As he defends his cruel act, Tamburlaine focuses on his cosmically ordained role of "Scourge of God and terror of the world" (IV.i.156), asserting, "these terrors and these tyrannies . . . I execute, enjoin'd me from above, / To scourge the pride of such as Heaven abhors" (IV.i.148–151). To Tamburlaine, Calyphas' weakness was one such abomination to the Gods.

Planning to terminate her life, Olympia presents Theridamas with the gift of an ointment which, she says, prevents the skin from being pierced. Offering to demonstrate its power, she instructs Theridamas to cut her neck, and she is slain. This episode recalls Tamburlaine's forceful seizure of Zenocrate in Part I, yet here, the fruits of Theridamas' pursuit suggests that love cannot be won by tyranny.

Tamburlaine abuses the conquered kings, who draw his chariot as they are whipped. He commands his men to move forward to Babylon.

In **Act V**, Tamburlaine brutally destroys Babylon. When Babylon's Governor's life is threatened, he quickly offers the city's hidden treasure in exchange for his safety. Cunningly, Tamburlaine takes the treasure and has the governor killed. He then demolishes the city, drowning the citizens and burning the books. Meanwhile, Callapine, struggling to hope for his own victory, plans with the King of Amasia to fight Tamburlaine.

The **final scene** of the drama portrays Tamburlaine's illness and death. Conceiving this illness as a war, Theridamas describes death battling against the spirit of Tamburlaine, as the "cowards invisibly assail his soul" (V.iii.13). Techelles offers a plea to the powers that have faithfully favored the Scythian leader, urging them to continue to honor his life. Usumcasane appeals to this God's pride, arguing that humans will understand Tamburlaine's death as a sign of the deity's own defeat. Tamburlaine himself speaks of the god that "seeks to conquer mighty Tamburlaine" (V.iii.43) and of the monster Death who "stands aiming at (him) with his murdering dart" (V.iii.69). Concluding that he fights in vain "against those powers that mean t'invest (him) in a higher throne" (V.iii.122), he examines a map of the world, marking his journeys, describing his conquests, and passing on his crown to his son. Gazing upon Zenocrate in her hearse, advising his son to continue in his rule, and finally, saying a simple farewell to his officers and friends, Tamburlaine dies. Amyras' cry, "Let earth and heaven his timeless death deplore, / For both their worths will equal him no more," concludes the drama (V.iii.253–4). ❖

List of Characters in
Tamburlaine the Great II

Calyphas, son of Tamburlaine, refuses to follow his father's path of martial ambition achievement. Boldly declaring to his brothers, "I know sir, what it is to kill a man; / It works remorse of conscience in me" (IV.i.27–28), he refuses to fight in the battle against the Turks. Tamburlaine, enraged and unable to tolerate his son's pacifist spirit, stabs and kills Calyphas.

Amyras, son of Tamburlaine, follows his brother Celebinus in asserting his desire to be a conqueror like his father. At the close of the play, Amyras succeeds Tamburlaine and is crowned. His words of grief and tribute to his father conclude the drama

Celebinus, son of Tamburlaine, is eager to become a warring conqueror like his father. Early in the play he tells the proud Tamburlaine, ". . . you shall see me, if I live, / Have under me as many kings as you," (I.iv.54–55). When his brother Calyphas is unwilling to fight in battle, he attempts to bring him onto the field, warning him that Tamburlaine will be furious if he does not fight.

Theridamas, King of Argier, is Tamburlaine's first ally in Part I of the play. In Part II his character takes on greater significance. Theridamas is the only character who dares to respond to Tamburlaine's overwhelming grief when Zenocrate dies. Theridamas falls in love with and pursues Olympia, and tricked by her, inadvertently slays his beloved.

Techelles, King of Fez, and loyal follower to Tamburlaine, presents Tamburlaine with Moors and other troops for the battle against the Turks. He is a key military leader in the battle and comforts and prays for Tamburlaine during his illness and death.

Usumcasane, King of Morocco, faithful supporter of Tamburlaine, presents Tamburlaine with soldiers for the fight against the Turks. He reports on his conquests in Guallatia, the coast of Spain, the Strait of Gibraltar, and Canaria. Like Techelles, he is a primary leader among Tamburlaine's men and is also present at his death.

Orcanes, King of Natolia, is betrayed when King Sigismund breaks his truce and fights against him. He prevails in battle and gives credit to Christ for his victory against the Christians, asserting that the Christian God would not validate Sigismund's treacherous act. He comes to the aid of Callapine, is defeated by Tamburlaine and held captive by him.

King of Trebizon, King of Soria, and the **King of Jerusalem** meet Callapine upon his escape and pledge their support. Conquered by Tamburlaine and subjected to cruel and humiliating treatment, these kings curse Tamburlaine and decry his "merciless, infernal cruelty" (IV.iii.85).

King of Amasia meets with Callapine after Tamburlaine has defeated the other kings. Assuring Callapine that they will conquer Tamburlaine, Amasia describes his vision of Mahomet, "Marching about the air with armed men, / To join with (Callapine) against this Tamburlaine" (V.ii.35).

Gazellus, Viceroy of Byron, advises Orcanes to make peace with Sigismund. Later he serves as a mediator between the two proud kings who offend each other in their diplomatic discussion.

Uribassa is an advisor to King Orcanes.

Sigismund, King of Hungary meets with Orcanes and offers peace or war, telling the Turkish King, "Take which thou wilt"(I.ii.3). He signs a truce with Orcanes, but later breaks it, on the basis that he does not need to keep his agreement with a non-Christian king. When he is defeated, he attributes the loss to a just God who is punishing him for his betrayal. He dies from a wound received in the battle.

Frederick and Baldwin, Lords of Buda and Bohemia, persuade Sigismund to break his truce with King Orcanes, arguing that they are not bound to agreements made with those in whom "no faith nor true religion rests" (II.i.34) and urging Orcanes to take the opportunity, "That God hath given to venge [the] Christians' death" (II.i.52).

Callapine, son to Bajazeth, watched his father and mother suffer under Tamburlaine's cruel tyranny and grew up suffering under his yoke. Fueled by the desire to avenge his family's suffering, Callapine escapes from his imprisonment and gathers numerous kings to battle with the aim of stopping the vicious conqueror. Tamburlaine perishes before he is able to respond to Callapine's and the King of Amasia's challenge to fight.

Almeda, Callapine's keeper, is persuaded by the prisoner to help him escape. At this time, Callapine promises Almeda numerous rewards, including a crown. Callapine keeps this promise, provoking Tamburlaine's rage by crowing Almeda before his eyes. Tamburlaine swears to "knock out his brains" after the battle (III.v.143).

Governor of Babylon is urged by Maximus and other citizens to surrender to Tamburlaine, but he refuses, calling them all "[v]illains, cowards, traitors to (the) state" (V.i.43). Yet, when Tamburlaine is ready to have him hung and shot, the Governor offers Tamburlaine hidden gold in exchange for his life. Tamburlaine takes the treasure and has a group of his soldiers shoot at him at once.

Captain of Balsera, wounded in battle against Techelles and Theridamas, dies beside his despairing wife Olympia.

Son of the Captain of Balsera witnesses the death of this father, and then instructs Olympia, "Mother, dispatch me, or I'll kill myself, / For think you I can live and see him dead" (III.iv.26–27)? She stabs him and he dies.

Zenocrate, wife to Tamburlaine, is a more developed and expressive character in Part II of the drama. She boldly articulates her frustrations with Tamburlaine's devotion to martial conquest, and urges her husband to be patient and forgiving with their young sons. Zenocrate falls ill and begs enraged Tamburlaine to accept her death, warning him that if she learns her death caused his own, her happiness in heaven will turn to despair.

Olympia, grieving wife of the Captain of Balsera, kills her son after her husband's death, and prepares to kill herself, desiring that her family's souls remain together. She is interrupted by Theridamas and Techelles who, against her will, take her with them to Tamburlaine. Theridamas declares his love for Olympia. Despairing Olympia wants to end her life and devises a trick whereby Theridamas accidentally slays her.

Tamburlaine, introduced as an ambitious Scythian shepherd in Part I, is in Part II a fierce Emperor ruling vast territories and enjoying fame as the "Scourge of God and terror of the world" (IV.i.156). In Part II, Tamburlaine suffers the loss of his beloved Zenocrate, whom he continues to worshipfully adore even after her death, keeping her interred body with him. Throughout the play, Tamburlaine is engaged in the project of indoctrinating his sons to become martial conquerors like their father. When Calyphas refuses to go to war, Tamburlaine kills his son, unable to accept his tranquil disposition. Falling ill in the final scene of the play, Tamburlaine passes his rule onto Amyras, and dies victorious, succumbing only to the gods and to human mortality. ❀

Critical Views on
Tamburlaine the Great II

G. Wilson Knight on Sadism and Idealism
in the Play

[G. Wilson Knight was Professor of English Literature in the
University of Leeds and President of the Leeds University
Theatre Group. He is the author of numerous classic works of
literary criticism on Shakespeare, including *The Wheel of Fire,*
The Imperial Theme, The Crown of Life, The Sovereign Flower,
and *The Shakespearean Tempest.* He has also authored books
on Milton, Swift, Pope, and several major Romantic poets.
Here Knight discusses the unresolved conflict between aesthetic idealism and sadism in Parts I and II of the drama.]

Elizabethan idealism does not tell the whole truth of the national
soul. Poetic refinement coexisted with barbaric cruelty; bear or bull
baitings, whippings, and hideously prolonged executions, were
sources of public delight. Christopher Marlowe faces this all too
human co-presence of sweetness and sadism with almost too
uncompromising an honesty.

The two parts of *Tamburlaine the Great* (*c.* 1587) show us the
Scythian conqueror rising from humble origin to world power. His
appearance is god like (1; II. i) and throughout he feels himself as
backed by cosmic energies. The sequence of conquests is repetitive and
would be boring were it not for the splendid verse. The poetry has fire
and fervour but little of Kyd's modulation; it rings rather than pul-
sates. There is imagery of sun, spheres and meteors and a glitter of
crowns and weapons. Of earth and its vegetation we hear little. Colours
are sharp. Proper names can be grand and geography, as so often in this
expanding age, an intoxication. Kingship is avidly apprehended:

> To wear a crown enchas'd with pearl and gold,
> Whose virtues carry with it life and death;
> To ask and have; command and be obeyed. . .

(1; ii. v.)

The lines on man's questing Renaissance intelligence, opening with

> Our souls whose faculties can comprehend

The wondrous architecture of the world,
And measure every wandering planet's course . . .

see this straining aspiration coming to rest in

That perfect bliss and sole felicity
The sweet fruition of an earthly crown.
(1; II. vii.)

The juxtaposition is a true reading of Renaissance ambition. Tamburlaine even aims to

march against the powers of heaven
And set black streamers in the firmament,
To signify the slaughter of the gods.
(2; V. iii.)

Such excess, near comedy, is saved by the strong rhetoric and also by a grim realism.

For there is no sentimentalizing. Though he can speak rhapsodies of aesthetic idealism such as the famous 'If all the pens that ever poets held . . .' (1; V. ii), Tamburlaine is quite ruthless; in him all chivalric values are reversed; his enemies he not only conquers but degrades. Bajazet, the Turkish king, is caged and mockingly treated as an animal, he and his queen providing indecent amusement for Tamburlaine and his followers (1; IV. ii, iv). A rebellious viceroy is to be bitted, 'harnessed', whipped, fed, and stabled like a horse (2; III. v). Tamburlaine enters in a chariot drawn by kings with bits in their mouths, whipping them (2; IV. iii). Others await their turn and their curses are stifled by the bits, Tamburlaine's boy engaging in the fun: 'How like you that, sir king? Why speak you not?' (2; IV. iii). Apart from these incidents, human beings are naturally here regarded as cattle: 'With naked negroes shall thy coach be drawn' (2; I. iii). More entertainment is provided by the hoisting up and shooting of the Governor of Babylon (2; V. i); sadism here is a matter less of causing pain than of reducing the victim's human dignity, or integrity. Whilst claiming god-like status for himself, Tamburlaine would render others ludicrous. Irrelevant extremes face each other in contrast to the spiritualized humanism of Lyly and Kyd. No doubt the first audiences roared with delight, but it is more than slapstick; it is a terrible revelation of an enduring human instinct. We are not invited, except by the sufferers, to criticize: there is no catharsis, the juxtaposition of idealism and sadism being left unresolved.

—G. Wilson Knight, *The Golden Labyrinth: A Study of British Drama* (London: Phoenix House, 1962): pp. 54–55.

D. J. PALMER ON TAMBURLAINE'S IDENTIFICATION WITH NATURE

[D. J. Palmer is the author of numerous books on English Literature, including *The Rise of English Studies: An Account of the Study of the English Language* and *Literature from Its Origins to the Making of the Oxford English School.* In this excerpt he argues that Tamburlaine's identification with nature, dramatized in Part I, is inverted in Part II of the drama.]

Tamburlaine's dazzling progress of conquest through the kingdoms of the earth in Part I of the play is dramatised as that of a prodigy in Nature. He is identified with natural forces; his wrath is like a storm at sea, his army like the stars in heaven; but most commonly he is compared to the meteors and comets that blaze across the sky, phenomena that keep no regular course like the perfect motions of the planets, or to the thunder and lightning, the force of Jove himself. Such violent images recall Lucan's description of Caeser, as Marlowe renders it, 'urging his fortune, trusting in the gods':

> So thunder which the wind teares from the cloudes,
> With cracke of riven ayre and hideous sound
> Filling the world, leapes out and throwes forth fire,
> Affrights poore fearefull men, and blasts their eyes
> With overthwarting flames, and raging shoots
> Alongst the ayre and nought resisting it
> Falls, and returnes, and shivers where it lights.
> (ll. 152–8)

In Part II, however, this identification of Tamburlaine with natural forces is inverted. With Zenocrate's death, Nature for the first time is at odds with the hero's will, and Tamburlaine can no longer see himself as fulfilling Nature's purposes. Instead he turns upon Nature itself, and whereas previously his earthly triumph was described in the imagery of the heavens, now by a significant rhetorical inversion, the imagery of battle and slaughter is transferred to the heavens themselves:

> I will persist a terrour to the world,
> Making the Meteors, that like armed men
> Are seene to march upon the towers of heaven,
> Run tilting round about the firmament,
> And breake their burning Lances in the aire,
> For honor of my woondrous victories.
>
> (ll. 3875–80)

These lines conclude the scene in which Tamburlaine has killed Calyphas, his cowardly son; an ironic episode, since the father shows himself no less unnatural than the son whose 'shame of nature' he has purged.

—D. J. Palmer, "Marlowe's Naturalism" in *Mermaid Critical Commentaries: Christopher Marlowe*, ed. Brian Morris (New York: Hill and Wang,1968): pp. 167–168

M. C. BRADBROOK ON THE DISTINCTIONS BETWEEN THE REPRESENTATION OF TAMBURLAINE IN PARTS I AND II OF THE PLAY

[M. C. Bradbrook's publications include *Elizabethan Stage Conditions; Themes and Conventions of Elizabethan Tragedy;* and *The School of Night, The Rise of the Common Player: A Study of Actor and Society in Shakespeare's England,* and *The Living Monument: Shakespeare and the Theater of His Time.* Here she discusses the evolution of Tamburlaine's character between Parts I and II of the play.]

Tamburlaine is in fact more like a pageant than the modern idea of a play. Its central theme (Tamburlaine's 'thirst of reign') is highly generalized, its speech is uncolloquial, its feeling dehumanized and its action conventional. But this does not prevent its being a good play in the Elizabethan manner. Regarded simply as an artistic success,

Tamburlaine, Part 1, is the most satisfactory thing Marlowe ever did, except *Hero and Leander*. But it could not be repeated. The sensuous intensity and emotional tenuity were only possible to an immature mind. Marlowe could not help developing, and so becoming more aware of personal feeling and of a wider range of sensuous impressions; he could not help his blank verse reflecting the increased development and becoming more varied and flexible too. So that in *Tamburlaine*, Part 2, he could not revive the conqueror of Part 1. The cumulative narrative could not be stretched any further, and the story of Part 2 is either a variation of Part 1 (the four kings being substituted for Bajazet) or a series of irrelevant incidents, such as those connected with Olympia. Marlowe's flagging interest is betrayed by the incorporation of passages from his current reading, in an undigested form (especially the speeches on military strategy, 3. 2). The characterization is also less consistent. Marlowe is in parts capable of a new tenderness to humanity, which does not fit in with the old figures. At the death of Zenocrate, when Tamburlaine says:

> For she is dead! thy words do pierce my soul;
> Ah, sweet Theridamas, say so no more:
> Though she be dead, yet let me think she lives,
> And feed my mind that dies for want of her—
> 2. 4. 125 ff.

there is, as Miss Ellis-Fermor notes, a development beyond the earlier play. Even the decision to burn the town where she died is made the occasion for a conceit which would have been out of place before, because based on a natural human grief.

> The houses, burnt, will look as if they mourned.
> 2. 4. 139 ff.

On the other hand the Tamburlaine of Part 2 falls below the earlier figure in some respects. His ends are more definite and less exalted. He even says:

> Cooks shall have pensions to provides us cates:
> And glut us with the dainties of the world.
> 1. 6. 92–3

The coarsely sensuous 'glut' indicates the new kind of feeling which has crept in. Marlowe cannot keep Tamburlaine's magnificence generalized any longer, nor can he keep the slaughter unreal and unmoving. There is a great deal of red, sticky blood in Part 2; it flows in the scene where Tamburlaine cuts his arm (3. 2. 115) and it is given through the verse. Battlefields are 'covered with a liquid purple veil' and 'sprinkled with the brains of slaughtered men' (1. 4. 80–1).

The finest passages of verse are those which point forward to *Faustus* and the later plays, or which depend on other writers—

> Helen, whose beauty summoned Greece to arms
> And drew a thousand ships to Tenedos—
>
> 2. 4. 87–8

or the reminiscence of Spencer (4. 3. 119–24). Marlowe is clearly uncertain of himself, and his verse reflects the transition. It is noticeable that he sometimes tries to pull it together by a use of strophic repetition, as in the famous 'To entertain divine Zenocrate' or the chronic lament of the three followers (5. 3) for the death of Tamburlaine. This scene opens with an echo of the earlier play.

> Now clear the triple region of the air. . . .
> Smile, stars that reigned at my nativity
> And dim the brightness of their neighbour lamps. . . .
>
> Part 1, 4. 2. 30 ff.

reappears as

> Weep, heavens and vanish into liquid tears!
> Fall, stars that govern his nativity
> And summon all the shining lamps of heaven
> To cast their bootless fires to the earth. . . .

Each of the three kings speaks in turn and each speech ends with a rhymed couplet. The same kind of pattern appears at the level of action in the scenes where the three kings deliver their crowns up to Tamburlaine (1. 4, 5): it is very like the entries of the lords in 3 *Henry VI*, 5.I.

There is on the whole little symbolic action in Part 2, the particular equipoise which made it possible in Part 1 having been destroyed. In his next play, Marlowe took a different type of narrative, and constructed his play in quite another fashion. . . .

—M. C. Bradbrook, "A Discussion of *Tamburlaine.*" In *Critics on Marlowe,* ed. Judith O'Neill (London: George Allen and Unwin, 1969): pp. 34–36.

HELEN GARDNER ON THE THEME OF HUMAN LIMITATION IN THE PLAY

[Helen Gardner held the Merton Professorship of English Literature at Oxford University. She is the editor and author of *The Art of T. S. Eliot; Divine Poems* and *Metaphysical Poets.* Here she discusses the play as an exploration of the limitations to man's control, focusing on Olympia's suicide.]

The theme of the first part of *Tamburlaine* is the power and splendour of the human will, which bears down all opposition and by its own native force achieves its desires. ⟨. . .⟩

The theme of the second part is very different. Man's desires and aspirations may be limitless, but their fulfilment is limited by forces outside the control of the will. There are certain facts, of which death is the most obvious, which no aspiration and no force of soul can conquer. There is a sort of stubbornness in the stuff of experience which frustrates and resists the human will. The world is not the plaything of the ambitious mind. There are even hints in the play that there is an order in the world, of which men's minds are a part, and that man acts against this order at his peril. This theme of the clash between man's desires and his experience demands a more complex structure for its expression that was demanded by the theme of the triumphant human will in the first part . . .

The third act opens with a scene which is obviously intended to parallel Act 1, scene 6. There, Tamburlaine, having summoned his subject kings, assessed his forces for the coming campaign: here, Callapine, having been crowned with his father's crown Emperor of Turkey, is told by his tributary kings what strength they can bring for the coming struggle with Tamburlaine. This scene shows Callapine at the peak of his power; the confederation against Tamburlaine is at its height. By contrast, Tamburlaine in the next scene is at his most dejected, celebrating the death of Zenocrate by the futile and savage burning of a town. Having lost his wife, he turns to his sons for consolation, only to find himself baffled by the weakness of Calyphas. His attention is distracted by the other two, who show a dutiful indifference to pain, but a hint is given here of another of those forces which hamper us in the execution of our ambitions, the resistance of other wills, which refuse to accept the parts we assign to them.

This theme is developed in a subsidiary episode, which has usually been regarded as mere padding, that of Theridamas and Olympia, the Captain's wife. In reading this episode, one recalls the parallel situation of the first part, when Zenocrate, captured as a prize of war, also charms her conqueror by her beauty. There the conqueror was as successful in love as in war and his captive responded to his passion before he spoke of it. Theridamas, the hero of this episode, is associated in our minds with Tamburlaine, as his closest friend and most loyal follower; his fortunes have followed those of his master. The rebuff he suffers here at the hand of Olympia, who prefers death to his love, and eludes him finally, when he seems to have absolute power over her, by a clever ruse, seems to reflect back on Tamburlaine himself.

The death of Olympia follows immediately upon the murder of Calyphas, which is itself an example of failure coming on the heels of success. Act 3 ends with a scolding match between Tamburlaine and the Turkish kings and in Act 4, scene I Tamburlaine wins his first great victory over Orcanes and his allies; but the moment of triumph is spoilt by the cowardice of Calyphas and he celebrates his victory by the murder of his son, whom he can kill, but cannot force to obey him. . . .

—Helen Gardner, "The Second Part of *Tamburlaine the Great*." In *Critics on Marlowe*, ed. Judith O'Neill (London: George Allen and Unwin, 1969): pp. 38–41.

C. L. Barber on Zenocrate's Death

[C. L. Barber (1913–1980) was professor of literature at the University of California, Santa Cruz, and Beckman Visiting Professor at the University of California, Berkeley. He was the author of *Shakespeare's Festive Comedy* and, with Richard P. Wheeler, *The Whole Journey: Shakespeare's Power of Development*. In this article he examines Tamburlaine's love for Zenocrate and his reaction to her death, analyzing the play from a Freudian perspective.]

The one great exception to the absence of tragic irony about the hero is the death of Zenocrate in *Part 2*. It provides a situation in which Marlowe can dramatize fully Tamburlaine's paradoxical dependence on her. The scene is constructed with splendid symmetry: static figures—three physicians, three warrior companions, three sons—are disposed around Zenocrate's bed of state to set off Tamburlaine's passionate movement. Everything turns on the moment when "*The musicke sounds, and she dies.*"

What concerns me here is the way the scene extends the rhythm of "conceiving" and "subduing." It opens with the most enlarged conceiving of Zenocrate, shifts after her death to the expression of extreme anguish of frustration, and then recovers with a characteristic subduing, by domineering, of the anguish of conceiving. Thus we can see in it both the creativity of the impulse to worship that Marlowe expresses and also the limitation that vulnerability in suffering beauty involves for him.

Tamburlaine begins his lament by describing Zenocrate as the source, now darkening, of all light and life, and then goes on to the superb lyric which describes the prospect of her assumption into heaven:

Now walk the angels on the walles of heauen,
As Centinels to warne th' immortall soules,
To entertaine deuine *Zenocrate.*

(2983–85)

In the beautiful lines which follow, there is, for once, deep reverence and a loss of self in contemplation of the harmony of the universe.

Instead of appropriating the cosmos to aggrandize his identity, Tamburlaine envisages for a moment welcome into heaven:

> The Cherubins and holy Seraphins
> That sing and play before the king of kings,
> Vse all their voices and their instruments
> To entertaine diuine *Zenocrate.*
> And in this sweet and currious harmony,
> The God that tunes this musicke to our soules:
> Holds out his hand in highest maiesty
> To entertaine diuine *Zenocrate.*
>
> (2994–3001)

Of course in making Zenocrate's death equivalent to the Assumption of the Virgin Mary, the lines on one side are blasphemous, and characteristically aggressive. But Marlowe's sensibility is reaching, through the figure of Zenocrate, out beyond the limitation of violence. Tamburlaine ends his speech by asking that an ecstasy take him up to heaven and end his life with Zenocrate's:

> Then let some holy trance conuay my thoughts,
> Vp to the pallace of th' imperiall heauen:
> That this my life may be as short to me
> As are the daies of sweet *Zenocrate.*
>
> (3002–5)

In expressing, through Zenocrate, something like religious awe, this beautiful poetry fits with a view that it is initially through the figures of the parents, godlike, as experienced in infancy, that men reach toward society's conceptions of divinity. Such a view need not deny the objective reality of the transcendent forces to which a mature worship responds. The parents after all themselves depend, in their creative and nurturing role, on forces and realities which transcend their individuality. Filial piety, in a successful development, goes beyond the parents to become a larger social and/or religious piety, whatever the forms under which it is envisaged. The Oedipus complex, in this perspective, appears as the route through which a child's worship may develop into a man's, or else be blocked or distorted. Tamburlaine's celebration of Zenocrate, and the impulse which goes with it to lose himself, with her, in the "currious harmony" of divinity, need not be reduced, by formula, to "nothing but the expression of oedipal feelings." The poetry captures, through her, actual majesty of the universe, whether in the imagery of light in the opening cosmological celebration of her eyes, or in the neo-Christian imagery of the assumption lyric.

—C. L. Barber, *Creating Elizabethan Tragedy: The Theater of Marlowe and Kyd* (Chicago: University of Chicago Press, 1988): pp. 68–70.

Plot Summary of
The Jew of Malta

In Malta, every alliance has its price, and all men are quick to betray each other in pursuit of greater profit. Machevill, representing the spirit of self-preservation, recites the Prologue and his spirit permeates the play. Most patently manifested in the brilliant villain Barabas, the other characters, often emblems of Christian hypocrisy, also consistently deceive and betray to further their own aims.

Barabas is most patently characterized as a wealthy man who loves his fortune above all else. Yet a closer reading reveals that Barabas is not merely a caricature of human avarice. Upon losing his fortune, Barabas compares his misfortune to that of a man who, "in a field amidst his enemies / Doth see his soldiers slain, himself disarmed" (I.ii.203–5). In Malta, Barabas is surrounded by his enemies, and as this passage suggests, his riches ensure the only kind of protection and power that he, as a Jew, may obtain. Ferneze's unjust seizure of his property thus constitutes the total destruction of Barabas' hard earned, gradually built, singular protection against a field of enemies—an anti-Semitic world.

In the **opening scene** of the drama, Barabas, Jew of Malta, joyfully counts his gold. He learns all Jews are required to attend a meeting in the senate house the following day. Barabas resolves to protect his wealth and himself, whatever should happen.

The Turks demand that Malta's tribute be paid and grant the governor one month to gather the funds. In one of the most subtly crafted scenes of the play, Governor Ferneze defends his order that the Jews give money for the tribute. Barabas responds with incredulity and sarcasm that rapidly grows into vehement protest and reasoned argument against the Governor's demand. Ferneze rules that each Jew must give half his estate, or convert to Christianity. All but Barabas quickly agree to concede half their possessions. When Barabas refuses, Ferneze seizes his entire estate and converts his home to a nunnery. This act constitutes the initial betrayal that sets in motion the action of the rest of the play.

When the officials depart, despairing Barabas addresses the other Jews: Why do they stand unmoved by his great loss and anger? Why did they so easily yield to the governor, leaving Barabas as sole opposition to his demands? In poignant poetry, Barabas laments this unjust loss. Recovering his composure by turning his thoughts to Abigail's welfare, he devises a plan to repossess money hidden in their home. Barabas reminds his daughter that "religion / Hides many mischiefs from suspicion" (I.ii.282–3), and Abigail persuades the Abbess to allow her in the home, now a nunnery, by pretending she desires to learn as a novice.

In **Act II**, Abigail retrieves the hidden riches. Martin Del Bosco, vice admiral to the King of Spain, arrives in Malta, hoping to sell slaves captured in his fight with the Turks. In order to sell the captives in Malta, he cleverly persuades Ferneze to break the league with the Turks, avoid the tribute, and be ruled by Spain. Del Bosco's strategy to leverage the political situation to increase his profit offers yet another manifestation of the Machiavellian spirit that permeates the drama.

The reader meets Barabas again in the slave market-place; he has rebuilt his fortune but habitually insults the "[u]nchosen nation, never circumcised" (II.iii.8) and the Governor who wronged him. Against the backdrop of the slave market where Don Mathias, Don Lodowick, Katherine, and other pious Christians peruse the human merchandise, Barabas fervently conceives a plan to destroy the emerging romance between Abigail and Don Mathias, and in so doing, work revenge on the Governor through his son Lodowick.

Barabas purchases the Turkish slave Ithamore and each man enthusiastically describes to the other the vile and vulgar crimes they have committed. Barabas contentedly concludes, " . . . We are villains both: / Both circumcised, we hate Christians both" (II.iii.216–7).

Barabas exacts revenge on the Governor by pitting Lodowick and Mathias against one another, playing off the jealous competition over Abigail already brewing between them. Fixated on achieving his aim, Barabas locks Abigail in the house so that she cannot interfere with his plot.

In **Act III**, Barabas' vengeful scheme is consummated, when Lodowick and Matthias, spurred by a false letter of challenge composed by Barabas, slay each other. From this point in the drama, his plots and evil deeds become inhumane and outrageous. When innocent Abigail learns of Mathias' death and deciphers her father's plan, she concludes, ". . . there is no love on earth, / Pity in Jews, nor piety in Turks" (III.iii.49–50) and joins the nunnery. Barabas learns of Abigail's betrayal and instantly shifts his affection to Ithamore, naming the slave "[his] love" (III.iv.14) and "[his] second life" (III.iv.15), adopting Ithamore as his only heir. But Barabas reveals his duplicity to the audience in an aside that Ithamore will "ne'er be richer than in hope" (III.iv.53). Barabas immediately begins to plot revenge and, captivated by this endeavor, carefully concocts a poisoned porridge for Abigail. Deluded with the hope that her death will ensure his inheritance, Ithamore willingly delivers the poison.

The entire nunnery consumes the porridge, inspiring the bizarre scene of a house full of ailing nuns, simultaneously offering their panicked, final confessions. Abigail admits to guarding the secret of her father's murderous plot against Matthias and Lodowick, explaining that she reveals her secrets not to punish her father, but only to earnestly confess her own sins. The friar Bernadine promises not to divulge this information, but soon reveals himself to be another example of Christian hypocrisy, when moments after her death, he resolves to threaten the Jew with this secret knowledge.

In **Act IV**, Bernardine goes to Barabas, who delivers a powerful performance, feigning great remorse for his deeds. Pledging to donate his wealth to whichever religious house will shelter and baptize him, Barabas uncovers the shallow piety of the friars, who quickly devolve into a jealous argument over whose religious house should receive Barabas' riches.

Barabas brilliantly plots revenge upon Bernadine, because the friar knows his secrets, and on Jacomo, whom he holds responsible for Abigail's conversion. Barabas and Ithamore coldly murder Bernadine and then, even more outrageously, fool Jacomo into thinking that he is responsible for Bernadine's death. Barabas gleefully mocks Jacomo, telling him he could never become a Christian; friars murder one another! Jubilant at the perfect execution of his scheme, Barabas then reports Jacomo to the law.

In need of money, the courtesan Bellamira and the thief Pilia-Borza flatter Ithamore and offer themselves at his service. They persuade Ithamore to demand money from Barabas, and the slave threatens to confess all if the riches are not provided. Pilia returns with the money and they send a second demand for further funds, which Barabas reluctantly provides. Angry, but no longer surprised by such self-serving treachery, Barabas disguises himself as a musician and embarks to see how Ithamore "revels with [his] gold" (IV.iii.67). Intending to kill them, Barabas offers Ithamore and the others poisoned flowers to smell. He is stunned to hear Ithamore entertaining his companions with patent lies about Barabas the Jew, who practices strange habits, living on "pickled grasshoppers" (IV.iv.59–60) and never changing his shirt. In the final act of the play, Barabas is caught: Bellamira and Pilia learn of Barabas' vicious acts from Ithamore and readily report his crimes to the Governor. To avoid being punished, Barabas drinks a sedative concoction that aids him in feigning death. Assumed to be deceased, Barabas is thrown outside the city walls. There he encounters the Turkish army, and seizes the opportunity to work revenge on all of Malta. He eagerly helps the Turks enter the fortified city.

The Turks prevail and appoint Barabas governor of Malta. Yet Barabas questions, "But Malta hates me, and in hating me / My life's in danger, and what boots it thee, / Poor Barabas, to be the Governor . . ."(V.ii.30)? For the first time Barabas crafts a plot which does not center around revenge. In order to win back friendship with Malta, Barabas offers to destroy the Turks, in exchange for money from the Governor. From his experience, Barabas has learned that a fortune, built alone and kept alone, does not ensure wealth or security. Ferneze agrees to his plan, and with great zeal, Barabas now physically crafts the trap for his victims. He provides a lavish feast for the Turkish army at a nearby monastery and during the meal, hidden cannons massacre the soldiers. At his home, Barabas has created a concealed device by which the floor opens, and will drop Calymath into a dangerous pit.

However, before the dining Turk plummets down, Ferneze betrays Barabas, trapping Barabas in his own device. Ferneze and Calymath refuse to help him, and Barabas dies in the pit, proudly proclaiming to both the plots he worked, and suffering he caused for each of them. After self-righteously boasting that he has generously saved Calymath's life, Ferneze reveals his underlying intentions, firmly declaring that he will keep Calymath as a prisoner in Malta. His unctuous self-congratulation and words of praise to heaven close the play. ❀

List of Characters in
The Jew of Malta

Machevill delivers the Prologue to the play. Understood to be an emblem of the spirit of treacherous self-interest and preservation, he opens the drama and his spirit permeates it throughout. Machevill proudly declares, "And let them know that I am Machevill, /And weigh not men, and therefore not men's words" (Prologue, 7–8). He comments on the numerous hypocrites who pretend to disdain him, remarking, "Admired I am of those that hate me most." Machevill also notes that Barabas' wealth "was not got without ⟨his⟩ means" (Prologue, 32).

Barabas, Jew of Malta, is the dynamic hero-villain and central focus if the play. The Barabas of the opening acts, though captivated by his gold and committed to his personal gain, is not a barbaric criminal. Only after Ferneze seizes his estate does Barabas become a vengeful character whose evil deeds grow more and more extreme throughout the drama. He works revenge on the Governor by bringing about the death of Ferneze's son; after he has murdered her beloved he avenges Abigail for joining the nunnery, murdering her with poison. Betrayed first by his slave Ithamore and then by the Governor whom he has helped, Barabas dies trapped in his own device, a pit intended for the Turkish leader Calymath. As he dies he urges himself to "end [his] life with resolution" (V.v.79) ardently describing the suffering he caused Calymath and the Governor, and cursing the "Damned Christians, dogs and Turkish infidels" (V.v.85).

Ferneze, the sanctimonious Governor of Malta, entertains the audience even as he infuriates them with his outrageous hypocrisy. He offers a skillfully crafted representation of self-righteous piety and smug duplicity. Unjustly seizing Barabas' estate, in one of the most powerful scenes in the drama, Ferneze remains unchanged, as calculating and cold in the final scene. After trapping Barabas in the pit, he proudly proclaims, "Now Selim note the unhallowed deeds of Jews: /Thus he determined to have handled thee, / But I have rather chose to save thy life" (V.v.91–3). Ferneze lets the perpetrator of these "unhallowed deeds" painfully die, while willingly using them to his own advantage.

Ithamore, Turkish slave to Barabas, cheerfully tells Barabas how he has spent his time: "In setting Christian villages on fire, / Chaining of eunuchs, binding galley-slaves. / One time I was an hostler in an inn, / And in the night time secretly would I steal / To travellers' chambers, and there cut their throats" (II.iii.205–209). Companion and dutiful servant to Barabas, Ithamore is eventually seduced by the flattery and beauty of cunning Bellamira, at whose instruction he demands money from Barabas.

Selim-Calymath the Turkish leader and son of the Turkish empire, demands that Malta's tribute be paid early in the drama, and returns to conquer with the aid of Barabas in Act V. He is ultimately held prisoner by Ferneze.

Callapine, is a Bashaw who arrives with Selim-Calymath in Act I, and returns to claim Malta's tribute in Act III.

Abigail, the pious and innocent daughter of Barabas, is the singular figure of virtue in the drama, who never schemes to gain money or power. Resolutely loyal to her father in the initial acts of the play, she breaks from him and her Judaism when she learns of Barabas' role in the death of her beloved Mathias. Though she converts to Christianity and joins a nunnery, she deliberately continues to protect her father by concealing his responsibility for the deaths of Mathias and Lodowick.

Don Lodowick, son of Governor Ferneze, is easily gulled by Barabas, who leads the young gentleman to believe that he will marry Abigail. Lodowick begins to treacherously compete against Mathias for Abigail's affection as soon as Mathias tells Lodowick of his newfound beloved.

Don Mathias possesses a genuine love for Abigail and she devotedly requites his affection. He describes her as "matchless beautiful" (I.ii.382) and "the sweetest flower in Cytherea's field" (I.ii.376). Mathias is tricked by Barabas' plot, which eventually leads to his death at the hands of Don Lodowick.

Katherine, mother of Don Mathias, reveals her vicious anti-Semitism by her cruel remarks against Barabas in the market-place. She mourns over the body of her slain son, swearing revenge with Ferneze on whomever was responsible for the enmity between Lodowick and Mathias.

Martin Del Bosco, vice admiral to the King of Spain, arrives in Malta with a ship of "Grecians, Turks, and Afric Moors" (II.ii.9) whom he captured after a fight against the Turkish fleet. He artfully persuades Ferneze, Governor of Malta, to break league with the Turks and come under the rule of Spain, so that he can sell the captured slaves in Malta.

Friar Jacomo converts Abigail to Christianity, and thus incites Barabas' rage against him. His religious hypocrisy is exposed when he easily succumbs to petty arguments over Barabas' riches with Friar Bernadine. Gulled by Barabas and Ithamore, he is held responsible for the murder of Bernadine.

Friar Bernadine, an emblem of religious hypocrisy in the play, hears Abigail's confession with feigned compassion, and then, moments after her death, exclaims his regret that Abigail died a virgin. He attempts to manipulate Barabas with the information he learned through Abigail's confession, but he is fooled by Barabas' feigned remorse and seduced by promises of his riches. Barabas and Ithamore murder Bernadine while he is sleeping.

Bellamira, a courtesan, first appears in Act III of the play. Unable to earn money while the town of Venice is besieged, she cunningly seduces Ithamore to gain access to Barabas' money. When Ithamore confesses Barabas' evil deeds to them, Bellamira and Pilia-Borza report them to the Governor.

Pilia-Borza, a thief in league with Bellamira, carries Ithamore's demands for money to Barabas. Barabas offers a wonderfully vivid description of him in Act IV: ". . . a shaggy tottering slave, / That when he speaks, draws out his grisly beard, / And winds it twice or thrice about his ear; / Whose face has been a grindstone for men's swords, / His hands are hacked, some fingers cut quite off; / Who when he speaks, grunts like a hog, and looks like one that is employed in catzerie" (IV.iii.6–11). ❀

Critical Views on
The Jew of Malta

U. M. ELLIS-FERMOR ON BARABAS AND THE
MACHIAVELLIAN SPIRIT

[Una Mary Ellis-Fermor was lecturer in English literature,
Bedford College, University of London. She served as the
General Editor of the New Arden Shakespeare and authored
*Frontiers of Drama; Christopher Marlowe; Jacobean Drama:
An Interpretation* and *Shakespeare the Dramatist*. In this
excerpt Ellis-Fermor discusses Barabas' acute suffering, and
his subsequent development into a Machiavellian figure.]

Barabas, at the opening of the play, is a man who has become powerful by the steady exercise of native tenacity and intelligence, without
being driven by a fierce or fanatic desire for power. Even at the height
of his fortunes, when his wealth is greater than that of all the other
Maltese merchants combined, he is not intoxicated by it. ⟨. . .⟩

⟨. . .⟩ It is only under pressure of extreme suffering, when the only
thing that he could have dreaded had come upon him through the
agency of the basest hypocrisy and injustice, that Barabas's mind
loses its balance, and ferocity and cunning gradually take possession
of it. Even so, his clear-sightedness does not at once desert him, and,
at the crisis of his fortunes, he is revealed as a man whose habit of
thought is honest, beset on all sides by trickery and hypocrisy shel-
tering themselves behind popular sentimentality and superstition.
He is deliberately trapped by the Governor and Knights of Malta and
the forfeiture of his goods, which had clearly been predetermined, is
glossed over with a repulsive parade of justice, through which he see
unerringly:

⟨. . .⟩ "Policie!" exclaims Barabas, left to himself, "that's their profes-
sion," and he adopts their own weapon, the only one remaining to
him. But he never deceives himself; he becomes perforce a Machiavellian in his tactics, not a blind hypocrite, as are his opponents:

⟨. . .⟩ And once adopted, the Machiavellian character suits him well,
for he is of a quick invention, steady nerves and resolute; under pressure of his wrongs he rapidly becomes implacable and unscrupulous.

⟨. . .⟩ In catastrophe he is not dismayed to find himself alone; it has not been his habit to hold himself referable to any other man:

> "No, I will live; nor loath I this my life:
> And since you leave me in the Ocean thus
> To sinke or swim, and put me to my shifts,
> I'le rouse my senses, and awake my selfe."
>
> Ll.501–4

He is indeed, as was Machiavelli's hero, and as were all of Marlowe's, "fram'd of finer mold than common men."

From this point a kind of a diabolical cunning takes possession of Barabas, which is not unworthy of the dignity of his first appearance, for his schemes are bold, astute, ruthless and successful. He becomes, for the brief extent of an act and a half, a satanist, but a satanist who rebels against a world-order of unclean and unjust things. The third and fourth acts are broken up into a series of intrigues, some of which follow on naturally from Marlowe's scheme in the first part, while some, such as the Bellamira episodes, seem to be contrary to that purpose. More significant, however, than this, which is at best doubtful evidence, is the lapse in Barabas's character, out of which all power and inspiration seems to have gone, except for a rare phrase or two in which the spirit of the second act is revealed. In the fifth act the character becomes recognisable again, some of the impressiveness of the earlier part returns to the play, and tactics that were begun then come to fruition. The intermediate steps in the development have been omitted, but the true Machiavellian emerges now and again from the confusion of the final act and suggests what would have been the nature of the acts in which Marlowe's work is less visible:

> "Thus loving neither, will I live with both,
> Making a profit of my policie;
> And he from whom my most advantage comes,
> Shall be my friend.
> This is the life we Jewes are us'd to lead;
> And reason too, for Christians doe the like."
>
> Ll.22.31–18

—U. M. Ellis-Fermor, *Christopher Marlowe* (London: Methuen & Co. Ltd., 1927): pp. 98–101.

Harry Levin on Barabas the Hero-Villain

[Harry Levin (1912–93), Irving Babbitt Professor of Comparative Literature at Harvard University, authored numerous books of literary criticism, including *James Joyce: A Critical Introduction* and *Contexts of Criticism* as well as *The Overreacher,* Levin's Study on Christopher Marlowe. In this excerpt, he discusses the *Jew of Malta* in relation to Marlowe's other plays, and examines Barabas in comparison to other Marlovian and Shakespearean heroes.]

Barabas the Jew is a man with a grievance, but his retaliation outruns the provocation. His revenges, augmented by his ambitions, are so thoroughgoing that the revenger becomes a villain. He is not merely less sinned against than sinning; he is the very incarnation of sin, the scapegoat sent out into the wilderness burdened with all the sins that flesh inherits. *Tamburlaine* dealt with the world and the flesh, but not with the devil; that was to be the sphere of *Doctor Faustus.* Somewhere between the microcosm of *Doctor Faustus* and the macrocosm of *Tamburlaine* stands *The Jew of Malta.* Contrasted with the amoral Tamburlaine, Barabas is an immoralist, who acknowledges values by overturning them. Contrasted with the devil-worshiping Faustus, he is more consistently and more superficially diabolical. His is a test case for the worldly logic, if not for the spiritual consequences, of the Satanic decision: "Evil be thou my Good" (*Paradise Lost,* IV, 110).

In Shakespeare, as critics have noted, it is the villains who expound free will and take a skeptical view of planetary influences. In Marlowe the villains are heroes, by virtue—or perhaps we should say *virtù*—of their unwillingness to accept misfortune. As soon as he is left "to sinke or swim" (503), Barabas defies his "lucklesse Starres" (495). Like Tamburlaine and the rest, he considers himself to be "fram'd of finer mold than common men" (453). His attitude toward others is that of Lorenzo, the villain of *The Spanish Tragedy:*

Ile trust my selfe, my selfe shall be my freend.
(III, ii, 118)

This fundamental premise of egoism is stated even more incisively by Richard III:

Richard loues *Richard,* that is, I am I.
(V, iii, 184)

Barabas makes the same affirmation, somewhat more deviously, by mis-quoting slightly from the *Andria* of Terence:

Ego mihimet sum semper proximus.

(228)

The articles of his credo have been more bluntly set forth in the pro-logue, where Machiavel makes a personal appearance to bespeak the favor of the spectators for his protégé. ⟨. . .⟩

The Jew of Malta, continuing Marlowe's studies in *libido domi-nandi,* emphasizes conspiracy rather than conquest—or, in the terms laid down by *Tamburlaine,* policy rather than prowess. From the roaring of the lion we turn to the wiles of the fox. "Policy," the shib-boleth of political realism, is mentioned thirteen times, and serves to associate Barabas with Machiavelli.

> —Harry Levin, *The Overreacher: A Study of Christopher Marlowe* (Cambridge, Massachusetts: Harvard University Press, 1952): pp. 60–61.

DOUGLAS COLE ON BARABAS AND THE TRADITIONAL "MORALITY VICE"

[Douglas Cole was Professor of English at Northwestern University. He is the author of *Christopher Marlowe and The Renaissance of Tragedy* and *Suffering and Evil in the Plays of Christopher Marlowe.* In this excerpt, Cole urges readers to view Barabas not as a naturalistic character, but as a sym-bolic representation of a particular brand of evil.]

Viewed from the perspective of a broadly naturalistic drama, a drama that makes some efforts at psychological realism or, at least, adequately motivated characterization, the Jew of Malta will always appear an inhuman and incredible creature. From the same point of view the vision of evil underlying the play must be judged as basi-cally a simplistic one: suffering and evil are not problems, but the result of sheer villainy on the part of totally selfish characters. Justice triumphs and evil is destroyed when the cunning traitor is cunningly betrayed. But there is a danger here that such a perspective and its consequent judgments are altogether too conditioned by presuppositions of the modern theater, and do not take into account the nature of the Elizabethan stage, which had firm roots in medieval traditions and modes of thought that long outlived Marlowe himself. The morality tradition, in which characters are not really persons but moral principles, or dramatic metaphors for moral principles, is particularly relevant in the case of *The Jew of Malta;* the character of Barabas begins to make more sense when the demand for psychological realism is relaxed and examination of the dramaturgical and moral principles which underlie his character is intensified. Such an examination must include the ideas involved in the labels affixed to the protagonist by Marlowe—Barabas as Jew, Barabas as Machiavel—as well as the characteristic dramaturgical qualities Barabas shares with the morality Vice.

⟨. . .⟩ What Marlowe has done is to cast in the form of the Vice's conventional exposition of his activities—which do not depend on mortal limitations of space and time—the characteristic evils with which the Jews were charged: poisoning, military exploitation, and usury. Barabas embodies them all. He shares with some Vices the provocation of his victims to despair and suicide, although his interest is not in spiritual damnation, but merely in the joy of destruction. This is indicative of the crucial difference in the Jew's career from that of the Vice: Barabas' goal is the material destruction of his enemies, not their spiritual ruin; he *is* not a morality Vice, he only acts like one. Such behavior, nevertheless, carries with it the inescapable quality of conscienceless inhumanity, since the Vice is essentially inhuman and needs no provocation other than his own nature for the evil he produces. Barabas' villainy, therefore, is largely gratuitous and thoroughly cold-hearted despite his appeals for "justice"; his speech to Ithamore makes plain that he needs no psychological motivation for his crimes. Lust for revenge and absolute egoism are suggested, but they really are not sufficient to account for such spectacular evil deeds.

Barabas makes a great point of hating Christians and plotting their destruction, but the course of the play makes it quite clear that he is equally malevolent and treacherous with everyone, Christian, Turk, or Jew, including his own villainous henchman and his own daughter. This is the Vice's characteristic of aggression against everyone else. Like the Vice, again, the Jew's career is essentially an exhibition of his villainies, most of which are brought about by artful deception. Barabas use the Vice's trick of weeping in order to persuade Mathias that the match of Abigail and Lodowick is an unhappy one as far as he himself is concerned: all part of the plot to set Mathias at odds with his friend. This setting people at odds with one another, occurring again with the two Friars, is a further characteristic activity of the Vice figure, and one in which Barabas, as well as Ithamore, delights.

—Douglas Cole, *Suffering and Evil in the Plays of Christopher Marlowe* (Princeton, New Jersey: Princeton University Press, 1962): pp. 131, 140–141.

WILBUR SANDERS ON FERNEZE'S SEIZURE OF BARABAS' WEALTH

[Dr. Wilbur Sanders' publications include *The Dramatist and the Received Idea: Studies in the Plays of Marlowe and Shakespeare, John Donne's Poetry* and *Shakespeare's Magnanimity*. He is currently a teaching fellow at Selwyn College, Cambridge University. In this excerpt, he offers a close analysis of Ferneze's seizure of Barabas' estate, focusing on the delicate changes in tone and sentiment that underlie the dialogue between the two characters.]

Part of the scene's mastery resides in the subtle gradations of tone— the elevation of moral sentiment varying directly with the speaker's rapacity, politeness being merely a function of greed, and innocence a preliminary affectation. Ferneze opens with suave urbanity— 'Hebrews, now come near'—and expostulates mellifluously—'Soft, Barabas! there's more 'longs to't than so'. The Jew counters with a pretended ignorance of their drift which pierces the euphemistic mist, and the First Knight, enraged by Barabas's feigned belief that they are asking him to fight in the army, explodes,

Tut, Jew, we know thou art no soldier;
Thou art a Merchant, and a money'd man,
And 'tis thy money, Barabas, we seek.

I. ii. 52

The swift transition, from surly contempt to an oily servility before the personification of Mammon, represents dramatic economy of a high order. Barabas's tone undergoes a complementary series of transformations: at first affected innocence ('How, my lord! My money!'), it modulates through mock incredulity to moral indignation ('The man that dealeth righteously shall live'), dying away finally in stoical indifference ('take it to you, i' the devil's name'). Ferneze, on the other hand, preserves a uniformly lofty tone—extortion is no occasion for indecorum—and is at some pains to cloak his expediency in moral rectitude. He offers the Jew the kind of supercilious mock-explanation that comes naturally to the consciously impregnable when dealing with a helpless victim.

His sophistries, however, expose in a lucid syllogism the logic of anti-semitism: Barabas will contribute to the Turkish levy, not 'equally', but 'like an infidel':

> For through our sufferance of your hateful lives,
> Who stand accursed in the sight of heaven,
> These taxes and afflictions are befall'n.
>
> I. ii. 63

Ferneze's primary intention is to justify the levying of the entire tax upon a tiny fraction of the population, but he cannot resist the additional gratification of a moral, as well as economic, vaunt: Observe, O Jew, the self-sacrificial charity of the Christians who, even at the risk of incurring the divine wrath, have graciously permitted Jews to trade in Malta. The logical form, with its *post hoc propter hoc* fallacy, is also characteristic: Jews are under a curse; we are suffering under the curse of Turkish extortion; *ergo* our misfortune is due to your accursed presence. If there were no more here than this syllogistic expediency, the comment would be perceptive. But the factor that lifts it out of the field of social commentary, and elevates it to the comic plane, is the lofty moral tone in which Ferneze chooses to enunciate his logical travesty. It is the timeless voice of pious dissimulation. ⟨. . .⟩

The scene is more than an essay in the dialectic of religious intolerance. Neither party is, in any case, greatly moved by the events that take place, both having taken the necessary decisions, and made the necessary arrangements, before this encounter took place. What Marlowe leads us to perceive behind the verbal and rationalistic fencing, is the perennial comedy of acquisition and the substratum of universal Machiavellism which makes nonsense of the division into Jew and Gentile.

—Wilbur Sanders, *The Dramatist and the Received Idea: Studies in the Plays of Marlowe & Shakespeare* (Cambridge: Cambridge University Press, 1968): pp. 46–47, 50.

CLIFFORD LEECH ON BLACK COMEDY IN THE PLAY

[Cofounder of the Graduate Center for the Study of Drama at the University of Toronto, and Chairman of English at the University College, Professor Leech (d. 1977) authored *The Dramatist's Experience with Other Essays in Critical Theory* and edited *Marlowe: A Collection of Critical Essays*. In this article, Leech analyzes Marlowe's comic craft and style, focusing on his expression of dark humor in *The Jew of Malta*.]

[T]he dominating effect of Marlowe's play is comic, despite its frequent deaths and its passionately searching comments on human behavior in society, and despite its final picture of Barabas in the boiling cauldron. Edward II dies in a humiliating fashion, but with a dreadful scream. Barabas, even as he boils, has the leisure to curse; we are kept at a considerable distance from the pain of it. If we cannot totally deny the horror, if there is a blackness here, yet we come away with a sense of comedy, which is indeed sharpened by the Christian Ferneze's smugness about the way things have turned out. Mortimer has to pay for Edward's death with his own life; Ferneze gets his governorship back by dispatching Barabas. We shudder a little, but think that getting away with things is the politician's *métier* in the rather dreadful but non-tragic world of this play's Malta.

All through Marlowe's work there is an undercurrent of comedy. It is to be found even in *Edward II*, though that is the most subdued, the grayest, of the plays. Even there, the humiliation of the Bishop of Coventry (I.i), and the boasting of Baldock (II.i) that he is, despite his puritan's garb, ready to stab when occasion serves, have their suggestions of dark humor. So, too, has many a discreet line in that play, as in Warwick's brutal answer to Gaveston's last request to see Edward: "The king of heaven perhaps, no other king" (III.i.16).

But in *The Jew of Malta* we find the full exuberance of Marlovian comedy, as perhaps we should in *The Massacre at Paris* if we had its full text. It is black enough, and it goes along with a sense of the tragic. The Jew, after all, is the most energetic and enterprising man here, the one who will not compromise, the one who utters such uncomfortable truths as his claim that each man must be judged by what he does, not by what his ancestors have doomed him to. Of course, there is irony here too, for Barabas offends grievously. Yet in this world of little men he is several inches taller than the rest, though he began as a man wanting only the security of riches and the company of his daughter Abigail. Marlowe, in a fairly strenuously anti-Semitic society, made the Jewess Abigail his one clear manifestation of virtue. She loves; and in this Malta she is a paragon. Doubtless Marlowe was having his fun at the expense of Elizabethan England, but he was well read and could be sincere in recognizing virtue in distant tribes. He also "places" the ethic of both Barabas and Ferneze by juxtaposing them with the emblem of goodness.

Here in Malta were the Jews that England had banished, and here on occasion were the Moslems that England feared but knew were a long way off. Christians and Moslems had appeared together in *Tamburlaine*, but there both were on the grand scale, even if Tamburlaine himself had to stoop to comic gestures and was finally subject to time and the frailty of generation, and even if Sigismund broke his oath and was destroyed by it. Now in Marlowe's *Jew* Christians and Turks and Jews are alike small, engaged in petty matters of profit and individual murder and the ransoming of a small Mediterranean island. In this shrunken world Marlowe treads delicately, keeping his balance between simple farce on the one side and grandiosity on the other. There are moments of plain farce, as in the Bellamira scenes, and moments of deliberately old-fashioned bombast, as in the Jew's boasting to Ithamore of his habitual and random indulgence in the art of murder. These things make Marlowe's Malta ludicrous; but there are also moments of frustration and anguish. The dramatist declares allegiance neither to the persecuted Barabas nor to the Ferneze who gives thanks to God for the continuation of Christian power in the island. He does not present it all as a matter of simple or ironic fun. He makes us realize that these are men, however ludicrous and cruel their actions may be. That they achieve no wisdom does not differentiate them from the grandest of tragic heroes. As in tragedy, moreover, the fact of death is not shirked here, though treated with some lightness. There is, after all, a sense of the tragic, along with the dark comedy of it all.

—Clifford Leech, *Christopher Marlowe: Poet for the Stage* (New York: AMS Press, 1986): pp. 173–174.

Plot Summary of
Dr. Faustus

The prologue apologizes that *Dr. Faustus* will not portray lofty stories of kingdoms, deities or other "audacious deeds" (Prologue, 5), but will center upon "Faustus' fortunes" (Prologue, 8). This opening implicitly acknowledges the desire of both the audience and the drama's central character to witness magnificent spectacles and grand events, a desire which constitutes a central theme of the play. The prologue then describes Faustus as scholar who "surfeits" on magic (Prologue, 25).

In the **opening scene** of the drama, Faustus reviews the disciplines that he has mastered, lamenting the limits of each. Reasoning that Philosophy, Medicine, Law and Divinity are insufficient to satisfy his rapacious hunger for knowledge, Faustus asserts of magic, "But his dominion that exceeds in this / Stretcheth as far as doth the mind of man" (60–61). Complicating the prologue's division of subjects grand and small, Faustus here affirms that the mind of man constitutes its own vast sphere. Indeed, a central concern of the play is the disjunction between the incredible aspirations and imaginations that the human mind can conceive and the disappointing realities they produce. Marlowe's drama examines this problem and explores notions of damnation and contrition, the thirst for knowledge, and the boundaries between the realms of the human and the divine.

Good and Evil Angels appear and counsel Faustus; the Good Angel urges Faustus to read scripture, the Evil Angel encourages Faustus to adopt magic and be "lord and commander" (1.77) of the earth. Intoxicated by the Evil Angel's tempting words, Faustus imagines spirits at his service, searching the earth for secret wisdom and exotic treasures. His colleagues Valdes and Cornelius, skilled practitioners of the black arts, muse with Faustus on a future in which he shall lack nothing.

In the **Second Scene**, two scholars encounter Faustus' servant Wagner and inquire where Faustus has been. In a witty repartee deriding Aristotle, Puritans, and academic jargon, Wagner explains that Faustus is dining with Valdes and Cornelius. The scholars suspect that Faustus has "fallen into that damned art" (2.31) and resolve to try to reclaim their friend.

71

In **Scene Three**, Faustus performs magical rites, praying to Lucifer and Gods of the underworld and successfully conjuring a devil, whom he commands to return in the guise of a Franciscan friar. Delighted by the devil's prompt execution of his demand, Faustus proudly exclaims of his skill at magic. The devil promptly tempers his exaltation, warning that he is a mere servant to Lucifer, Prince of Hell, and is subject to Lucifer's desires. Mephastophilis further deflates Faustus' hopes, explaining that Faustus' blasphemy, and not his artful spells, summoned the devil; when the devils hear someone abjure the scriptures and Christ, they "fly in hope to get his glorious soul" (3.50).

Faustus readily proclaims his allegiance to Lucifer, and asks Mephastophilis about hell. Explaining that he conspired with Lucifer, an angel banished from heaven for his "aspiring pride" (3.68), Mephastophilis asserts that he resides in hell wherever he goes, tormented by the knowledge of his irreversible mistake. Though Faustus witnesses Mephastophilis' misery, he ignores what it portends, and resolutely orders Mephastophilis to inform Lucifer that he will surrender his soul in exchange for Mephastophilis' servitude.

In **Scene Four**, Faustus' boy Wagner and the Clown jest in the street. Their remarks, played out in the comic register, echo the central plot of the play. Wagner remarks that the clown is so poor that "he would give his soul to the devil for a shoulder of mutton" (4.8–9). Wagner promises the Clown that in exchange for his servitude, Wagner will teach the Clown to turn himself into "a dog, or a cat, or a mouse, or a rat, or any thing" (4.57–58).

In **Scene Five**, the central conflict of the play begins to unfold, as Faustus is repeatedly disappointed by the fruits of his agreement with the devil, and as the devil's limitations are successively revealed. Faustus is seized by fear when, at Mephastophilis' command, he stabs his arm in order to seal the agreement in his blood, and the blood does not flow. Faustus suspects that his soul is unwilling to sign the bill. Mephastophilis helps the blood to clear and, to appease the distressed Faustus, conjures dancing devils offering gold crowns. Seduced by this display, Faustus offers the written agreement to the devil, reading aloud the conditions it details: Faustus will be a spirit, Mephastophilis will be his invisible servant and appear at his command. In exchange, Faustus gives his soul to Lucifer and after twenty-four years, will eternally abide in hell.

Faustus' first priority, belying his worry of what is to come, is to query his servant about hell. Though Mephastophilis explains that he is tortured in a hell that follows him wherever he goes, Faustus, cavalierly replies that hell does not exist. His request for a wife, again reveals Mephastophilis' limitations: since marriage is a sacred bond, the devil is prohibited from providing a wife. Faustus requests books about the cosmos, but this leads to further disillusionment; his demand to know who created the world is answered only by Mephastophilis explanation that he is forbidden to utter the name of God. As Faustus is seized by doubts, Lucifer himself arrives and distracts Faustus with a colorful pageant of the Seven Deadly Sins. Faustus is temporarily satisfied by witnessing this delight.

In **Scene Six**, Robin the ostler has stolen one of Faustus' conjuring books, and imagines the mischief he will work with these spells at his command. In **Scene Seven**, Mephastophilis takes Faustus to Rome where, invisibly, they entertain themselves by playing outrageous tricks on the Pope and his friars, leaving the pious men singing a panicked dirge. In the following scene, Robin uses a magical spell to conjure Mephastophilis to deal with a Vintner accusing Robin of theft. Infuriated that he's been summoned merely to further Robin's amusement, Mephastophilis transforms Robin and Rafe into an ape and dog.

Chorus three describes Faustus' increasing fame and travels throughout the world. In **Scene Nine**, Marlowe presents Faustus at the height of his power; having been invited to the court, Faustus conjures Alexander the Great and his paramour for the Emperor. As a knight mocks him at the court, the reader witnesses a more personal use of his magic; Faustus has horns implanted on the Knight's head to avenge his offense. These trivial amusements, the height of what Faustus' magic can provide, reveal the futility and tedium of Faustus' existence.

Anxious that time is running out, Faustus desires to go to Wittenberg. His choices to return to familiar territory, and to go by foot, past a "fair and pleasant green" (9.98), suggest that he longs to enjoy the simple blessings that require no magic.

In **Scene Ten**, nearing the end of his life, Faustus is tormented by moments of anguish, but avoids them by turning to the pointless project of selling his possessions, cheerfully gulling a horse-courser who buys his magically created horse. **Scene Eleven** strongly echoes the action of **Scene Nine**; Faustus entertains a Duke and Duchess with his magic. This repetition in the action of the play further underscores the idleness and uniformity of his days. Wagner's observation that Faustus spends his final days carousing and banqueting with the students again suggests that Faustus refuses to face the reality of his impending eternity in hell. In the following scene, at the scholar's request, Faustus summons Helen of Troy and they marvel at her magnificence.

Urging Faustus to repent, an Old Man describes an angel hovering above Faustus' head, waiting to pour grace into his soul. An apprehensive Mephastophilis threatens to torture his body, and persuades Faustus to reaffirm his vow. With the hope that Helen's "sweet embracings" (12.76) will "extinguish clean" his doubts, Faustus summons her to be his paramour. Should Faustus' frailties tempt the reader to conclude that man is unable to resist temptation, Marlowe presents a contrasting figure in the Old Man. The devils enter to try this man's faith, but by his piety and conviction, he banishes them from his presence.

In the play's **final scene**, ailing Faustus despairs of his fate, and reveals his pact with the devil to his horrified colleagues. In his last hour, Faustus tries to repent, yet again is tormented by the fear of Lucifer's punishment. Faustus begins to frantically grasp at ways to escape his imminent doom, hysterically entreating the mountains to fall upon him and hide him, commanding the earth to open and harbor him, imagining his soul taking on some other form of life, and finally, as the devils enter, crying that his soul be changed to water drops hidden in the ocean. The devils enter and take a screaming Faustus away to hell.

The **epilogue** admonishes the audience to "[r]egard his hellish fall" (Epilogue, 4) concluding that it will, "exhort the wise / Only to wonder at unlawful things" (Epilogue, 5–6), but "entice forward wits to practice more than heavenly power permits" (Epilogue 8). ❀

List of Characters in
Dr. Faustus

Dr. John Faustus is the learned scholar who, consumed by a rapacious desire for knowledge and enticed by the power magic would bring, begins to practice the black arts. He sells his soul to Lucifer in exchange for twenty-four years of service from the spirit Mephastophilis. Disappointed and disillusioned by what the bargain actually provides, Faustus is repeatedly racked by fear and regret, but cannot repent. The damned doctor fails to be penitent and at the end of the drama, is taken by devils to hell, where he will eternally abide.

Wagner, student and servant to Faustus, provides comic interludes, particularly in his witty dialogues with the scholars and the clown early in the play. As the chorus, he also provides the audience with key observations about Faustus throughout the play.

Valdes and **Cornelius,** magicians and friends to Faustus, encourage him to take up magic and promise that their magical books will bring him great fame, power, and riches. He remarks that their words have "won (him) at the last," suggesting that they have long been trying to persuade him to take up magic. (Scene 1, 101)

The Good Angel first appears in Scene 1, urging Faustus to read Scripture and leave the book of magic aside. Reappearing later in the play, he tells Faustus that it is never too late to repent, and discredits Mephastophilis' threats.

The Evil Angel supports Faustus in taking up magic, telling him it will make him "on earth as Jove is in the sky" (Scene 1, 76). He encourages Faustus to shift his thoughts from heaven to honour and wealth. When the Good Angel instructs Faustus to repent, he counters that God could not pity him.

Mephastophilis, the devil conjured by Faustus, remains his companion and servant throughout the drama, carrying out Faustus' commands and sharing with Faustus the secrets of the cosmos. Banished from heaven after conspiring with Lucifer, Mephastophilis explains that he is in hell wherever he goes, tortured by his regret at willingly giving up the joys of heaven. Though openly sharing his misery with Faustus, Mephastophilis also aims to assuage Faustus' recurrent doubts about his pact with Lucifer.

Lucifer, Prince of Hell, explains Mephastophilis, is the "arch regent and commander of all spirits." (Scene 3, 64) He was the most dearly loved angel of God who, because of "aspiring pride and insolence" was expelled from Heaven. (Scene 3, 68) When Faustus cries out to Christ, Lucifer appears and tells Faustus, "Christ cannot save thy soul" (Scene 5, 259). Urging him to think of the devil, and not of God, Paradise or Creation, Lucifer presents to him a pageant of the Seven Deadly Sins.

Belzebub arrives with Lucifer when he presents the pageant of the Seven Deadly Sins.

Old Man enters toward the close of the drama, urging Faustus to "Break heart, drop blood, and mingle it with tears, / Tears falling from repentant heaviness . . ." (Scene 12, 30–31). He describes to Faustus an angel offering to pour "precious grace" into his soul. After Faustus has reaffirmed his vow to Mephastophilis, the old man returns, decrying accursed Faustus' miserable existence. The devils enter and the old man concludes that God is trying his faith. He boldly responds, "My faith, vile hell, shall triumph over thee!" and the devils leave him. (Scene 12, 106) ✤

Critical Views on
Dr. Faustus

[An eminent critic, journalist, and essayist, William Hazlitt
(1778–1830) published several books of dramatic criticism, including the classic *Characters of Shakespear's Plays*.
Here he provides a sweeping description of the play and its
central character, focusing particularly on Faustus' desires
to extend his power and knowledge beyond natural
boundaries.]

Marlowe is a name that stands high, and almost first in this list of
dramatic worthies. He was a little before Shakespear's time, and has
a marked character both from him and the rest. There is a lust of
power in his writings, a hunger and thirst after unrighteousness, a
glow of the imagination, unhallowed by any thing but its own energies. His thoughts burn within him like a furnace with bickering
flames; or throwing out black smoke and mists, that hide the dawn
of genius, or like a poisonous mineral, corrode the heart. His Life
and Death of Doctor Faustus, though an imperfect and unequal performance, is his greatest work. Faustus himself is a rude sketch, but it
is a gigantic one. This character may be considered as a personification of the pride of will and eagerness of curiosity, sublimed beyond
the reach of fear and remorse. He is hurried away, and, as it were,
devoured by a tormenting desire to enlarge his knowledge to the
utmost bounds of nature and art, and to extend his power with his
knowledge. He would realise all the fictions of a lawless imagination,
would solve the most subtle speculations of abstract reason; and for
this purpose, sets at defiance all mortal consequences, and leagues
himself with demoniacal power, with 'fate and metaphysical aid.' The
idea of witchcraft and necromancy, once the dread of the vulgar and
the darling of the visionary recluse, seems to have had its origin in
the restless tendency of the human mind, to conceive of and aspire
to more than it can achieve by natural means, and in the obscure
apprehension that the gratification of this extravagant and unautho-
rized desire, can only be attained by the sacrifice of all our ordinary
hopes, and better prospects to the infernal agents that lend them-

selves to its accomplishment. Such is the foundation of the present story. Faustus, in his impatience to fulfil at once and for a moment, for a few short years, all the desires and conceptions of his soul, is willing to give in exchange his soul and body to the great enemy of mankind. Whatever he fancies, becomes by this means present to his sense: whatever he commands, is done. He calls back time past, and anticipates the future: the visions of antiquity pass before him, Babylon in all its glory, Paris and Œnone: all the projects of philosophers, or creations of the poet pay tribute at his feet: all the delights of fortune, of ambition, of pleasure, and of learning are centered in his person; and from a short-lived dream of supreme felicity and drunken power, he sinks into an abyss of darkness and perdition. This is the alternative to which he submits; the bond which he signs with his blood! As the outline of the character is grand and daring, the execution is abrupt and fearful. The thoughts are vast and irregular; and the style halts and staggers under them, 'with uneasy steps';—'such footings found the soul of unblest feet.' There is a little fustian and incongruity of metaphor now and then, which is not very injurious to the subject.

> —William Hazlitt, "On the Dramatic Writers contemporary with Shakespeare, Lyly, Marlow, Heywood, Middleton, and Rowley." In *The Collected Works of William Hazlitt*, ed. A. R. Waller and Arnold Glover (London: J. M. Dent & Co., 1902): pp. 202–203.

HARRY LEVIN ON THE RELATIONSHIP OF MEPHASTOPHILIS AND FAUSTUS

[Harry Levin (1912–93), Irving Babbitt Professor of Comparative Literature at Harvard University, authored numerous books of literary criticism, including *James Joyce: A Critical Introduction* and *Contexts of Criticism* as well as *The Overreacher,* Levin's Study on Christopher Marlowe. Here Levin explores the relationship between Faustus and Mephastophilis, arguing that Mephastophilis is not merely a servant, but a dynamic companion to Faustus.]

Mephostophilis does nothing to lure Faustus on; he suffers for him, he sympathizes with him, above all he understands him; and, through this understanding, we participate in the dramatic irony. Faustus persists in regarding his fiendish attendant as a sort of oriental slave of the lamp, and Mephostophilis ironically promises more than his temporary master has wit to ask. Some day, after one fashion or another, Faustus will be "as great as *Lucifer*" (484)—he will arrive at the kind of ambiguous greatness that Fielding would attribute to Jonathan Wild. In the interim he shrugs:

> Come, I thinke hell's a fable. (559)

To which the suffering spirit replies with the bitterest of all his ironies:

> I, thinke so still, till experience change thy minde. (560)

For Faustus, even more than for Edward or Barabas, the fruit of experience is disillusionment. As soon as the contract is signed and sealed, he is eager to resolve ambiguities, to satisfy the cosmic questions that teem in his brain. He is keenly aware that there are more things in heaven and earth than the trivium and the quadrivium; but his discussions with Mephostophilis scarcely proceed beyond the elementary data of natural history and the unquestioned assumptions of Ptolemaic astronomy. "Tush," Faustus cries impatiently, "these are fresh mens suppositions" (667). To the more searching inquiry, "Who made the world?" (677) his interlocutor must perforce be silent, since fiends are interdicted from naming God. When various books of occult and pseudo-scientific lore are provided, Faustus nervously thumbs through the black-letter pages, only to realize that he has exchanged his soul for little more than the quiddities of Wittenberg: "O thou art deceiued" (610). In his undeception he listens to the conflicting angels again, and again the Evil Angel outargues the Good. Faustus, at all events, is beginning to respect the grim silences of Mephostophilis. Now it becomes the latter's task to divert him, but each diversion turns out to be a snare and a delusion. Faustus, being "wanton and lasciuious, . . . cannot liue without a wife" (574). This demand is frustrated, as the *Faustbook* emphasizes, because marriage is a sacrament; whereas, for Mephistophilis, it is "a ceremoniall toy" (583). The best that

Mephostophilis can provide is equivocally diverting: *"a diuell drest like a woman, with fier workes."*

—Harry Levin, *The Overreacher: A Study of Christopher Marlowe* (Cambridge, Massachusetts: Harvard University Press, 1952): pp. 117–118

G. WILSON KNIGHT ON TENSIONS BETWEEN RENAISSANCE IDEALISM AND CHRISTIAN THEOLOGY IN THE PLAY

[G. Wilson Knight was Professor of English Literature in the University of Leeds and President of the Leeds University Theatre Group. He is the author of numerous classic works of literary criticism on Shakespeare including, *The Wheel of Fire, The Imperial Theme, The Crown of Life, The Sovereign Flower,* and *The Shakespearean Tempest.* He has also authored books on Milton, Swift, Pope, and several major Romantic poets. Here he examines Helen's appearance in *Dr. Faustus,* and analyzes the play as an exploration of the conflict between the incompatible religious and secular values of the era.]

Perhaps what most interests him is the Renaissance itself and all that it stands for, and this is his subject in *Doctor Faustus* (c. 1590–2), written round a third form of the power quest: magic. In dramatizing a revolt from medieval theology this extraordinary work sets the type for a long mythology of future Faust plays. The conception is vast, involving the conflict of two cultures, but the working out is disturbing. Dissatisfied with the unnatural constrictions of theology, Faustus solicits the aid of the devil Mephistophilis, whose gifts include the imaginative treasures of ancient Greece:

> Have I not made blind Homer sing to me
> Of Alexander's love and Oenon's death,
> And hath not he that built the walls of Thebes,
> With ravishing sound of his melodius harp,
> Made music with my Mephistophilis?
>
> (II. ii.)

Helen appears: 'Was this the face that launch'd a thousand ships?' (V.i). Aligned with these superb poetic excursions are Mephistophilis' offer of whores, and chaste maids, too, for his lust, with a deliberate repudiation of marriage (II.i). Renaissance idealism appears to be one with vice and both are from the Devil: instinct is simultaneously inflamed and condemned, and man trapped. Faustus is given great powers, and performs marvels, including materialization of the dead, his magic at this early stage in Europe's history blending occult practices with a symbolization of scientific advance in the centuries to follow:

> And what wonders I have done, all Germany can witness, yea all
> the world; for which Faustus hath lost both Germany and the
> world, yea Heaven itself . . .
>
> (V. ii.)

Once only, in this quiet prose, does Marlowe touch a Shakespearian tragic dignity. And retribution and self-abasement swiftly follow: 'See, see, where Christ's blood streams in the firmament' (V. ii). Devils take Faustus to Hell and a choric figure moralizes.

Even when the poetry of Faustus' agonized self-conflict is great, its virtues remain those of a dramatic monologue and in total structure the drama is fragmentary. The middle scenes, with the show of Deadly Sins and the cheap comedy of Faustus' practical jokes on the Pope, sag. The dramatized conflict is one of cultural externals without penetration to that centre from which alone a coherent action can mature. Renaissance and Christianity are not merely opposed; they are in desperate incompatibility; the drama itself endures the conflict it should harmonize. Poetry, vice, the occult and science stand on the one side and religion on the other, in mutual exclusion. Aiming at both 'tragedy' and 'morality' Marlowe achieves neither, whilst nevertheless bestriding the centuries like a Colossus. In *Doctor Faustus* two ages clash. ⟨. . .⟩

His people do not grow, as do Shakespeare's, through suffering. Tamburlaine becomes more and more repellent, the Jew disintegrates, Edward II is embarrassingly pathetic; and even Faustus' final declamation is no more than a sublime expression of terror. In Marlowe the most exquisite apprehensions are associated with the lascivious; he seems to be tormented by things at once hideously suspect yet tormentingly desirable; and he leaves us simultaneously aware of intoxication and degradation. His feminine interests are slight, and where there is humour it is cruel. He forecasts both Jonson and Milton and what he reveals is vastly important and deeply true. Yet revelation and truth are only half the tragic dramatist's task; the other half is transmutation, or catharsis, and this he does not master. His reach, admittedly titanic, exceeds his grasp.

—G. Wilson Knight, The Golden Labyrinth: A Study of British Drama
(London: Phoenix House, 1962): pp. 56–59.

A. BARTLETT GIAMATTI ON THE ROLE OF SUBPLOT IN THE PLAY

[A. Bartlett Giamatti (1938–1989) taught Italian, English, and comparative literature at Princeton and Yale Universities. He served as President of Yale and published several books, including *The Earthly Paradise and the Renaissance Epic* and *Exile and Change in Renaissance Literature*. In this excerpt he examines the merging of plot and subplot in *Dr. Faustus*.]

The function of a subplot is to burlesque the concerns of a main plot by mirroring those concerns in lower form; not simply to reduce mighty concerns to absurdity but also to show us that no man's mighty self is immune to human fallibility, to foolishness, to flaw. The subplot is the great equalizer, savagely reducing or gently jesting the main concerns as the dramatist sees fit. ⟨. . .⟩

⟨. . .⟩ The seemingly simple contrast of subplot and main plot leads back to the central problem of the play: how the power to shape—language—can also misshape. And we have been led to this because the clown, transformed, is only a version of what Faustus, mighty magician, will become.

Or, indeed, what Faustus is rapidly becoming before our eyes. For here is that ever-growing split between Faustus' mighty words and his trivial deeds, between the shapes his language envisions and the shapes it actually creates. ⟨. . .⟩

And when, over the course of the play, we see what Faustus does with those splendid powers; when we see how Faustus only uses them to vex the Pope and his retinue (III.i–ii), produce a dumb-show and put horns on a courtier (IV.ii), fool a fop with a false head (IV.iii) and a horse-courser with a false horse and leg (IV.v), and gather grapes for a pregnant Duchess (IV.vii)—then we see that what Faustus does with his power totally undercuts what we heard Faustus claim for his power. But not only does the power to be a god make trivia; much worse, that very power makes Faustus trivial. Over the play, the magician metamorphoses himself to a court jester, a fool. The process dramatized in the language of Act I.i is dramatized in the spectacle of the whole play.

The overall effect of this process is to trivialize everything, finally to trivialize main plot to the level of subplot. We see this happening when the characters of the subplot begin to enter the main plot—Wagner entering after Faustus gulls the horse-courser; Robin and Dick talking to the horse-courser and carter about Faustus' mighty deeds, like turning horses to hay. This merging of the two levels of life is completed in IV.vii when, after Faustus brings off his last piece of tremendous trivia—grapes for the Duchess—Robin, Dick, and Company burst in and one by one Faustus charms them dumb. Now subplot is main plot; there is no difference. With his power to gain a deity, Faustus has reduced the world to its lowest level. Instead of learning the secrets of the universe, he has turned reality to farce. Finally, even the power of language, the power of transformation, is itself dramatically trivialized before our eyes when, without a word, Faustus denies the gulls the power of speech. That mighty power of language is so abused it no longer even communicates on a simple level; it only produces silence in the mouths of fools.

—A. Bartlett Giamatti, "The Arts of Illusion" in *Christopher Marlowe*, (New York: Chelsea House, 1986): pp. 117–119.

C. L. Barber on the Limits to Tragic Effect in the Play

[C. L. Barber (1913–1980) was professor of literature at the University of California, Santa Cruz, and Beckman Visiting Professor at the University of California, Berkeley. He was the author of *Shakespeare's Festive Comedy* and, with Richard P. Wheeler, *The Whole Journey: Shakespeare's Power of Development*. In this excerpt, Barber discusses the way in which the tragic effect of the drama is mitigated as the play moves away from the protagonist's motives and towards a more distant understanding of his weaknesses.]

There is a limitation about Doctor Faustus as a tragedy, however, that goes with its ending and the attitude expressed in the author's postscript. The tragedy has turned into something like—too like—a scapegoat ritual: let the hero carry off into death the evil of the motive he has embodied, ridding it from the author-executioner and the participating audience. The final chorus pulls back from the hero to the relief of conventional wisdom:

> *Faustus* is gone, regard his hellish fall,
> Whose fiendful fortune may exhort the wise,
> Onely to wonder at vnlawful things,
> Whose deepenesse doth intise such forward wits,
> To practise more than heauenly power permits.
> (1481–85)

Beyond the limiting moral perspective of the chorus, we have seen in detail, notably in the final soliloquy, how the fate of the hero is integral with his motive. But it is a motive that, in its dreadful consummation, has lost all connection with the willed heroic alternative that gave it value as a rebellious quest for pleasure, beauty, power.

Faustus's increasing, finally total helplessness in the grip of his motive is part of the play's limitation. Partly this is the effect of his egotism and alienation and the limited realization of a social world around him. The moment of greatest human pathos, as his end approaches, comes when he is with the scholars: ⟨. . .⟩

Here, in some of the most effective writing in the play, is the only moment when Faustus feels the loss not of his own soul, or of heaven for his soul, but of human society: "Ah my sweete chamber-fellow! Had I liued with thee, then had I liued stil, but now I die eternally. . ." (1359–60). But it is pathetic rather than tragic: the loss Faustus expresses is for a kind of fulfillment that he has neither sought nor left behind in his heroic enterprise. ⟨. . .⟩

More full-hearted tragedy presents a protagonist committed to his heroic motive, on terms that he establishes, right through to the end—which in a tragic situation is his end. ⟨. . .⟩

In *Doctor Faustus,* by contrast, the failure of the final choric judgment to locate the protagonist's heroic significance in a larger human context reflects Faustus's withdrawal from his own endeavor. With Faustus we miss, after the opening scene, heroic commitment to the motive at the base of his identity. Instead we are shown his frantic efforts to escape identity.

There is a devastated feeling at the close of *Doctor Faustus,* in my experience almost shattering. None of the strange feeling *for* life comes through at the end, such as we get in Shakespeare (though perhaps less in *Coriolanus* than in any other major tragedy). Snow has suggested that the center of feeling in *Doctor Faustus* is somehow outside the central conflict, displaced by the gap that opens between "the phenomenological contours of the play" and Faustus's consciousness. Perhaps one can say that it moves more and more away from the protagonist as his helplessness and the play's understanding of it increase. *Tamburlaine* is limited by Marlowe's identification with a protagonist who himself dominates others by "conceiving and subduing both." In the more complex action of *Doctor Faustus,* identification gives way to the ever-widening distance the author puts between himself and what in him animates his protagonist. As Marlowe's Latin postscript boasts, it is another instance of "conceiving and subduing both."

—C. L. Barber, *Creating Elizabethan Tragedy: The Theater of Marlowe and Kyd* (Chicago: University of Chicago Press, 1988): pp.127–130.

A. D. Nuttall on the Paradox of Predestination in the Play

[Scholar A. D. Nutall is the author of *Crime and Punishment: Murder as a Philosophic Experiment* and the widely lauded study of Shakespeare, *A New Mimesis*. In this excerpt, he argues the problematic doctrine of predestination is a central, underlying concern of the play.]

Let us take from Act I, scene i, the speech in which Faustus rejects the study of theology, using what Luther calls 'the Devil's syllogism'.

> Jerome's Bible, Faustus, view it well.
> *Stipendium peccati mors est.* Ha! *Stipendium, etc.*
> The reward of sin is death? That's hard.
> *Si pecasse negamus, fallimur,*
> *et nulla est in nobis veritas:*
> If we say that we have no sin
> We deceive ourselves, and there's no truth in us.
> Why then belike we must sin,
> And so consequently die.
> Ay, we must die, an everlasting death.
> What doctrine call you this? *Che sarà, sarà,*
> What will be, shall be? Divinity, adieu!
>
> (A text, I. i. 38–49)

Faustus is reasoning from scripture, from Romans 6: 23 and I John I: 8: 'For the wages of sin is death' and 'If we say that we have no sin, we deceive ourselves, and truth is not in us.' ⟨. . .⟩

By Calvinist doctrine, Faustus's reasoning is straightforwardly applicable to man in his natural state, that is, to all not in receipt of grace, to all those who have not been elected by God for heaven. The First Epistle of John says that if we acknowledge our sins God will forgive us, and this appears to allow a significant moral initiative to human beings—something *we* can do, to get out of the hole we are in. But this initiative is, in its turn, very precisely removed by Calvinism.

Protestants were at first cheerful about the new doctrines. The fact that all are sinful suddenly did not matter: *no one* got to heaven by merit: one had only to acknowledge one's sinfulness and all was well. Then it was noticed that the modest act of acknowledging sin looked awfully like a virtuous action. Now the major premiss of

Calvinism is that man is totally depraved and therefore any truly virtuous action will have been initiated by God's grace. Of ourselves we can do nothing. This means that you need grace before you can make any proper acknowledgment of your sin. In effect, the door we thought was open has been shut in our faces. It is no longer open to each of us to find salvation by confession and repentance. Those predestined to damnation *cannot* properly acknowledge their sins. 〈. . .〉

Faustus's reasoning is wrong if he has been chosen by God, but the very fact that he is saying such things is a mark of non-election, in which case his reasoning is impeccable. The knot has now tightened. It is not just than sinful behaviour is a sign that one is predestined to eternal damnation. The sin of despair is here embodied in an exact and truthful statement of the underlying theology. There but for the grace of God go we.

In the 1616 text the Good Angel says, 'Never too late, if Faustus will repent.' It has been pointed out that this looks like a softening of the harder, more Calvinist reading of the 1604 text, 'Never too late if Faustus can repent' ('will' replacing 'can', II. iii. 81). Michael Keefer writes, 'Enfolded in that conditional clause is the brute question of fact on which the doctrine of double predestination hinges. If Faustus is going to be able to repent, then he is eternally out of trouble and it is never too late; but if he cannot, it will always have been too late.' 〈. . .〉

In the ordinary dramatic sequence of *Dr Faustus* this turns into a sort of chronological nightmare, producing a faint sense that time is somehow running backwards, undoing the marks of goodness in Faustus. Act II, scene iii (A text) begins with the words, 'When I behold the heavens then I repent', present tense. Glory be, we *hear* repentance affirmed by Faustus. But eleven lines later we have, 'I will renounce this magic and repent'. The present tense, which might have seemed to secure the present mercy of God, has become a future tense, and God's mercy is so much the further off. Five lines later the future tense becomes a (still fainter) conditional 'God will pity me if I repent'. Then, only two lines after that, we find, 'My heart's so hardened I cannot repent' (II. iii. 18).

As Faustus's heart hardens, the doctrine of predestination hardens round him, like concrete. I have said that a medieval person might well be puzzled that one who clearly wishes he had not done what he has done, and calls on Christ, should nevertheless be damned. If the contrition is missing that may be, as we saw, because God, not Faustus, has hardened Faustus's heart. This is all painful enough, yet it is given a further twist at V. ii. 26 ff. The 'third scholar' says, 'Yet Faustus, call on God', and Faustus answers, 'On God, whom Faustus hath abjured? On God, whom Faustus hath blasphemed? Ah my God, I would weep, but the devil draws in my tears. Gush forth blood instead of tears, yea life and soul!' By the law of moral extremes meeting in Calvinism the first two sentences look less like absence of contrition than a contrition so extreme that it merges with the sin of despair—as if Faustus is morally ashamed to call on God. Yet the third sentence actually begins with the words, 'Ah my God'. In context this cannot be a mere expletive. It must be a prayer. Faustus, having said that he is too enmeshed in sin to call on God, then succeeds in doing just that. Still, Faustus cannot weep. Is there anyone left who will infer from this physical restraint that Faustus was not really sorry at all?

We are watching the conclusion of a tragedy—that is to say, a death which is not bleakly deserved but is in some way terrible. It is terrible because the narrative of just punishment for sin is fused with another narrative of predestined damnation and future everlasting torture. Calvin was very willing to say that God is terrible but would never say that he is wicked—only that he is inscrutable. Marlowe conversely finds in the terror of God a space for moral criticism, a space for the special blasphemy of Christian tragedy.

—A. D. Nuttall, *The Alternative Trinity: Gnostic Heresy in Marlowe, Milton, and Blake* (Oxford: Clarendon Press, 1998): pp. 36–41.

Plot Summary of
Edward II

Marlowe's *Edward II* utilizes the historical account of a mutinous time and a neglectful King's reign to create a drama that examines not only human duplicity and ambition, but the subtle evolutions of motives and allegiances which, constantly shifting, shape all human experience, amplified and intensified in the court of Edward II. The play is also a story of human vulnerability, yet, Edward's chief weakness lies precisely where his vivacity and power resides. His reckless drive to cultivate and cling to all that he loves, while denying and ignoring the malice that surrounds him is both his greatest weakness and his most compelling attribute. The play leaves the reader with the feeling that Edward's tragic end results not from his personal flaws, but from the unhappy marriage of his circumstances and his temperament.

Upon his accession, Edward II recalls to England his beloved Gaveston, exiled by Edward I. Arriving at the court, Gaveston secretly listens as the nobles express their disapproval of his return. Mortimer Senior demands of the King, "If you love us, my lord, hate Gaveston" (I.i.79). Dismissing their admonitions, Edward ecstatically greets Gaveston in a celebratory reunion.

Act I portrays the escalating animosities between the nobles and Edward, unfolding both the lords' duplicity and the complex character of the King. The nobles' simmering hostility intensifies as they learn that Gaveston has been granted eminent political titles and that the Bishop of Coventry, responsible for Gaveston's exile, has been sent to the Tower at Gaveston's command. They gather and, led by Mortimer Junior, vilify Gaveston, "swoll'n with venom of ambitious pride" (I.ii.31) whom they fear will be "the ruin of the realm and [the nobles]" (I.ii.32). Queen Isabella enters, lamenting that the king ignores her while he "dotes upon the love of Gaveston" (I.ii.50). Yet she urges the nobles not to revolt, as she would rather suffer "a melancholy life" (1.2.67) than see Edward endure a rebellion.

The nobles seize Gaveston as Edward, stunned by their insolence, exclaims, "Was ever king thus overruled as I" (I.iv.37)? They present Edward II with a choice to approve Gaveston's banishment or suffer an insurrection. His political power far less dear to him than his beloved, Edward offers the nobles his kingdom, but they are not placated. Edward concedes and, sorrowing, escorts Gaveston away, banishing from the court the unhappy Queen, whom he holds responsible for failing to reconcile the nobles. Further distressing the Queen, Gaveston openly suggests that she is having an affair with Mortimer Junior. Desperate to win back the favor of the King, Isabella takes her plight to the nobles and conferences privately with Mortimer Junior. Marlowe leaves ambiguous the contents of this exchange, but Mortimer subsequently persuades the nobles to recall Gaveston, hinting that they could murder him if he is in England.

Mortimer Senior advises Mortimer Junior to accept Gaveston's presence, noting the many great kings who have "had their minions" (I.iv.390). Mortimer's reply offers a direct explication of his enmity for Gaveston. He reveals that Edward's doting on one of low birth, his squandering of the country's riches on Gaveston, and the pair's habit of flouting the nobles aggrieves him. Mortimer does not acknowledge what the drama itself illustrates—the problem of Gaveston provides an opportunity for an insurrection, and thus for Mortimer's rise to power.

In **Act II**, the lords' mounting resentment turns to action. In the opening scene, they describe their mutinous plot to the King in metaphors that only thinly veil their intentions. Infuriated at their disrespect but unable to impede their revolt, Edward indulges in a brief and blissful reunion with Gaveston. The nobles' sarcastic hostility provokes a defiant Gaveston, who is wounded by Mortimer. Edward hides Gaveston, hoping to ensure his safety. When Edward refuses to ransom Mortimer Senior, captured by the Scots, he further incites Mortimer Junior's indignation. Kent, brother to Edward II, begins to believe that Gaveston is a danger to the realm and defects with the Nobles.

Isabella cries out in grief and speaks of her love for Edward. As the nobles pursue Gaveston, Edward II helps him escape. Isabella, no longer attempting to placate Edward II by carrying out his demands, reveals Gaveston's location to Mortimer, in the hopes that she will end her misery by destroying the source of her husband's volatile passions. Marlowe begins to reveal the budding connection between Mortimer and the Queen, who remarks to "sweet Mortimer" (II.iv.59) that she "could live with [him] forever" (II.iv.60).

The lords seize Gaveston, but at the king's request, Arundel and Pembroke escort Gaveston to see Edward before his death. Not all of the nobles are so willing to risk their prisoner, however, and Pembroke and Arundel are ambushed by Warwick, who has Gaveston killed.

In **Act III**, Spencer Junior urges Edward to deal harshly with the mutinous nobles, and Edward concedes that he has previously responded too mildly to them. Unmoved by the news that King Valois has seized Normandy, Edward dispatches Isabella and the Prince to deal with Valois, brother to the Queen.

Edward learns of Gaveston's death and, stirred by the encouragement of his new companion, Spencer Junior, vows with unprecedented resolution to punish Gaveston's killers. Victorious after a battle against the nobles, Edward rails against the captive lords for their unlawful murder of Gaveston, executing the nobles and sending Mortimer to the Tower.

In **Act IV**, Kent, appalled by his brother's slaughter of the noblemen, helps Mortimer escape from the tower. They travel to France to join Isabella and the Prince.

Learning that Mortimer and the Queen "intend to give King Edward a battle in England" (IV.iii.36), Spencer Junior and Edward eagerly set out to fight. Taking up arms against his brother, Kent is seized by guilt, but resolves to feign fidelity to Mortimer to protect his own life. Revealing the calculated treachery of Mortimer and Isabella, he reasons, "Dissemble or thou diest; for Mortimer /And Isabel do kiss while they conspire" (IV.v.21–22). With a cool satisfaction, Isabella, victorious after the battle, makes the prince Lord Warden of the realm.

Hindered by a storm as they fled to Ireland, Edward, Spencer and Baldock find safety in a monastery. Calling Baldock and Spencer to discuss philosophy with him, Edward exclaims, ". . . this life contemplative is heaven- / O that I might this life in quiet lead" (IV.vi.20–21)! In this moment the reader glimpses the life that Edward, fundamentally indifferent to diplomatic affairs and alienated from his role as King, might have happily enjoyed were he born into a different circumstance. Rice AP Howell, a Mower and the Earl of Leicester surprise the escapees, arresting Baldock and Spencer and taking Edward to Killingworth.

Act V portrays Edward's imprisonment and his murder. Jailed at Killingworth, Edward vacillates, agreeing and then refusing to yield his crown. Swayed by Leicester's threat that the Prince will lose his right to the throne, Edward, with uncontrollable grief, capitulates to their demands. The Prince receives the crown, but is controlled by Mortimer, upon whom Isabel bestows the role of official Protector to the young king.

In **scene two**, Marlowe fully exposes Mortimer and Isabella's calculated treachery. Mortimer triumphantly declares, "Fair Isabel, now we have our desire . . . Be ruled by me and we will rule the realm" (V.ii.1, 5). The Queen replies, "Sweet Mortimer, . . . Conclude against [Edward II] what thou wilt, /And I myself will willingly subscribe" (V.ii.15, 19–20). Discovering that Edmund plots to free the King and hearing that Berkeley, Edward's keeper) has begun to pity him, Mortimer transfers Edward II to the watch of Matrevis and Gurney, instructing them to treat him callously. After conferring with Kent, the Prince, awakening to Mortimer's duplicity and dark aims, demands to see his father. Meanwhile, Edward II grows increasingly disoriented and miserable as he is shuttled between Killingworth and Berkeley, starved, and kept in the thick stench of dungeon air. Kent's attempt to rescue the king utterly fails.

Mortimer resolves to covertly bring about the King's murder. To conceal his intent, he composes an unpunctuated Latin letter, which can be read, either as "Fear not to kill the king, 'tis good he die" (V.iv.9) or "Kill not the king, 'tis good to fear the worst" (V.iv.12). Mortimer then employs Lightborn, a professional killer, to murder the King.

Mortimer commands the guards to execute Kent. Prince Edward protests but Mortimer sternly overrules him and the Prince wonders of his Protector Mortimer, "What safety may I look for at his hands / If that my uncle shall be murdered thus" (V.iv.108-9)?

Lightborn ingratiates himself to Edward, claiming that it is "[f]ar from [his] heart" (V.v.46) to do the king harm. Edward is certain of Lightborn's murderous intent but deludes himself in an attempt to find some comfort in his final hours. Lightborn murders Edward by pushing a spit up his anus. Carrying out Mortimer's orders, Gurney then stabs Lightborn.

Edward III, enraged by the news of his father's death, emerges in the final scene of the play with a ferocious energy and commanding power never seen before in the Prince, or in his father. Pursuing his rage to its end, seizing his rightful authority and demanding with utter conviction that justice be wrought, he has Mortimer executed and Isabella sent to the Tower. Offering Mortimer's head to his deceased father, Edward III mourns and declares, "Sweet father here, unto thy murdered ghost, / I offer up this wicked traitor's head; / And let these tears distilling from mine eyes/Be witness of my grief and innocency" (V.vi.99–102). ❀

List of Characters in
Edward II

Edward II, King of England, is a volatile, passionate and compelling figure whose complex personality is gradually revealed throughout the course of the drama. Though erratic, and often unjust, he wins the sympathy of the readers, inspires the adoration of Gaveston and Spencer Junior, and even softens his keepers into pity for him when captive at Killingworth. In the opening acts of the play, Edward II disregards the nobles' threats of insurrection and falls prey to their plots. After his beloved Gaveston is murdered he is a far more active and resolute leader, defeating the nobles in battle and having them executed. Yet Edward fails to escape their conspiracy and, by Mortimer's treacherous plot, is brutally murdered while imprisoned.

Isabella, Queen of England, wife to Edward II, and sister to the king of France, initially exhibits only complete devotion and love for her husband, who cruelly flouts her and rejects her affection. As the drama unfolds, she develops into a cunning conspirator and adulteress who plots, with Mortimer, to murder Edward II.

Prince Edward, the son of Isabel and Edward II, is a naïve child throughout most of the drama, but begins to suspect his mother and Mortimer in the closing acts of the play. Assuming that he will be easy to manipulate, Mortimer and Isabella plot to have the young boy crowned king. Yet they underestimate the Prince's courage and resolution; after Edward II is murdered, Edward III sharply perceives their conspiracy and has Mortimer executed and Isabella imprisoned in the tower.

Edmund, Earl of Kent, brother to Edward II, is at first stalwartly supportive of the King. But, realizing that the nation suffers because of Edward's adoration of Gaveston, Kent defects with the nobles, assisting in Mortimer's escape from the tower. Struck with guilt, he is compelled to support his brother once again. He is executed after being captured during an attempt to free Edward II from prison.

Mortimer Senior at first demands that Edward II banish Gaveston, but later advises Mortimer Junior to let Edward have his minion. He is captured in Scotland and Edward's refusal to ransom him gives Mortimer Junior further provocation to revolt from the King.

Mortimer Junior inflames the nobles' resentment toward Gaveston, and, once their mutinous plot is set in motion, takes advantage of it to further his own rise to power. A stern and cunning figure, Mortimer becomes the official Protector of Edward III when the young boy is crowned. While engaging in an adulterous affair with Isabella, he covertly plots Edward II's murder, employing Lightborn to kill him. At the close of the play, Edward III has Mortimer executed.

Earl of Leicester and **Bishop of Winchester** speak with Edward II when he is initially imprisoned, pressuring him to yield his crown. They threaten that Edward III will lose his right to the throne if Edward II does not willingly surrender his title.

Earl of Warwick, loath to risk losing Gaveston after the nobles have finally seized him, surprises Pembroke and Arundel as they escort Gaveston to see the King. He then has Gaveston killed.

Earl of Pembroke, willing to grant King Edward's request to see Gaveston once before his beloved is murdered, agrees to accompany Arundel and Gaveston, in order to further ensure that the captive Gaveston will be returned to the nobles.

Earl of Arundel requests that the nobles release Gaveston, allowing him to visit with the King before his death. Arundel reports Warwick's ambush and Gaveston's seizure to Edward II.

Earl of Lancaster, mutinous nobleman, plots with Warwick, Mortimer, and the other lords to bring about Gaveston's death.

Piers Gaveston, beloved of Edward II, was exiled to France by Edward I. Recalled to England when Edward II inherits the crown, Gaveston incites the hostility of the nobles, who are infuriated by Edward's doting upon him. Bold and witty, Gaveston answers the noble's sarcastic remarks about his low birth with a wonderful reply: "Base leaden earls that glory in your birth, / Go sit at home and eat your tenants' beef, / And come not here to scoff at Gaveston" (II.ii.74–76). Seized by the nobles, Gaveston is murdered in Act II.

Lady Margaret De Clare, heir to the Earl of Gloucester, is betrothed to Gaveston and briefly appears in Acts II and III of the play, traveling with Spencer Junior and Baldock to the court.

Spencer Senior, father to Spencer Junior, devotedly offers his allegiance and martial support to Edward II and in Act III, fights with the king against the nobles. Rice AP Howell turns in a captured Spencer Senior to Mortimer and Isabella and he is executed.

Spencer Junior plans to go to the court to serve Gaveston, reasoning that by serving the Earl of Cornwall, he will have the opportunity to win the favor of the King. Despite the fact that his initial aims involve some ambitious scheming, Spencer is quickly won over by Edward and becomes his loyal supporter and companion. When Gaveston is killed, Edward II adopts Spencer as his new favorite, bestowing political titles upon him.

Baldock, learned tutor to Lady Margaret, becomes the close companion of Edward II and Spencer Junior. He is arrested in the monastery with Spencer Junior. As Spencer Junior despairs of Edward's imprisonment and impending death, Baldock counsels, "To die, sweet Spencer, therefore live we all; / Spencer, all live to die, and rise to fall" (IV.vi.110–111).

Gurney and Matrevis, henchmen to Mortimer Junior, are the final guards of Edward II. As Mortimer has instructed them, they force Edward to endure harsh conditions, assist Lightborn in murdering the king and then slay the assassin. Gurney flees and Mortimer allows Matrevis to take flight as well. When Edward III gains possession of the letter ordering the King's death, Mortimer concludes that Gurney has betrayed him.

Lightborn, a depraved professional killer, is employed by Mortimer Junior to murder Edward II. He devises the covert, brutal means by which the king will be killed. First deceiving the king with pretense of pity and kindheartedness for the tortured prisoner, Lightborn viciously murders Edward II, stabbing a spit up his anus. By Mortimer's orders, Lightborn is slain by Gurney and Matrevis. ❀

Critical Views on
Edward II

[An eminent critic, journalist, and essayist, William Hazlitt
(1778–1830) published several books of dramatic criticism,
including the classic works *Characters of Shakespear's Plays;
Lectures on The Dramatic Literature in the Age of Elizabeth;*
and *Round Table: A Collection of Essays on Literature, Men
and Manners.* In this excerpt, he discusses the dramatic
weaknesses of the play as a whole, but praises Edward's
moving death scene, as well as other select passages.]

Edward II. is, according to the modern standard of composition,
Marlowe's best play. It is written with few offences against the
common rules, and in a succession of smooth and flowing lines.
The poet however succeeds less in the voluptuous and effeminate
descriptions which he here attempts, than in the more dreadful
and violent bursts of passion. Edward II. is drawn with historic
truth, but without much dramatic effect. The management of the
plot is feeble and desultory; little interest is excited in the various
turns of fate; the characters are too worthless, have too little
energy, and their punishment is, in general, too well deserved, to
excite our commiseration; so that this play will bear, on the whole,
but a distant comparison with Shakespear's Richard II. in conduct,
power, or effect. But the death of Edward II. in Marlow's tragedy, is
certainly superior to that of Shakespear's King; and in heart-
breaking distress, and the sense of human weakness, claiming pity
from utter helplessness and conscious misery, is not surpassed by
any writer whatever.

> '*Edward.*   Weep'st thou already? List awhile to me,
> And then thy heart, were it as Gurney's is,
> Or as Matrevis, hewn from the Caucasus,
> Yet will it melt ere I have done my tale.
> This dungeon, where they keep me, is the sink
> Wherein the filth of all the castle falls.
> *Lightborn.* Oh villains.

<pre>
Edward.   And here in mire and puddle have I stood
           This ten days' space; and lest that I should sleep,
           One plays continually upon a drum.
           They give me bread and water, being a king;
           So that, for want of sleep and sustenance,
           My mind 's distempered, and my body 's numbed:
           And whether I have limbs or no, I know not.
           Oh! would my blood drop out from every vein,
           As doth this water from my tatter'd robes!
           Tell Isabel, the Queen, I look'd not thus,
           When for her sake I ran at tilt in France,
           And there unhors'd the Duke of Cleremont.'
</pre>

There are some excellent passages scattered up and down. The description of the King and Gaveston looking out of the palace window, and laughing at the courtiers as they pass, and that of the different spirit shewn by the lion and the forest deer, when wounded, are among the best.

—William Hazlitt, "On the Dramatic Writers contemporary with Shakespeare, Lyly, Marlow, Heywood, Middleton, and Rowley." In *The Collected Works of William Hazlitt,* ed. A. R. Waller and Arnold Glover (London: J. M. Dent & Co., 1902): p. 211.

ALGERNON CHARLES SWINBURNE ON EDWARD'S DEATH AND MARLOWE'S INFLUENCE ON SHAKESPEARE

[Algernon Charles Swinburne (1837–1909) is best known for his poetry but also composed brilliant essays of literary criticism, many of which are collected in his *The Age of Shakespeare* which covers numerous playwrights, including Webster, Martson, Middleton and Marlowe. In the passage below, he lauds Edward's death scene, and argues that Marlowe had a positive and profound influence upon Shakespeare.]

The first great English poet was the father of English tragedy and the creator of English blank verse. Chaucer and Spenser were great writers and great men: they shared between them every gift which goes to the making of a poet except the one which alone can make a poet, in the proper sense of the word, great. Neither pathos nor humour nor fancy nor invention will suffice for that: no poet is great as a poet whom no one could ever pretend to recognise as sublime. Sublimity is the test of imagination as distinguished from invention or from fancy: and the first English poet whose powers can be called sublime was Christopher Marlowe. ⟨. . .⟩

In 'Edward the Second' the interest rises and the execution improves as visibly and as greatly with the course of the advancing story as they decline in 'The Jew of Malta.' The scene of the king's deposition at Kenilworth is almost as much finer in tragic effect and poetic quality as it is shorter and less elaborate than the corresponding scene in Shakespeare's 'King Richard II.' The terror of the death scene undoubtedly rises into horror; but this horror is with skilful simplicity of treatment preserved from passing into disgust. In pure poetry, in sublime and splendid imagination, this tragedy is excelled by 'Doctor Faustus'; in dramatic power and positive impression of natural effect it is as certainly the masterpiece of Marlowe. It was almost inevitable, in the hands of any poet but Shakespeare, that none of the characters represented should be capable of securing or even exciting any finer sympathy or more serious interest than attends on the mere evolution of successive events or the mere display of emotions (except always in the great scene of the deposition) rather animal than spiritual in their expression of rage or tenderness or suffering. The exact balance of mutual effect, the final note of scenic harmony between ideal conception and realistic execution, is not yet struck with perfect accuracy of touch and security of hand; but on this point also Marlowe has here come nearer by many degrees to Shakespeare than any of his other predecessors have ever come near to Marlowe. ⟨. . .⟩

The place and the value of Christopher Marlowe as a leader among English poets it would be almost impossible for historical criticism to over-estimate. To none of them all, perhaps, have so many of the greatest among them been so deeply and so directly indebted. Nor was ever any great writer's influence upon his fellows more utterly and unmixedly an influence for good. He first, and he alone, guided Shakespeare into the right way of work; his music, in which there is no echo of any man's before him, found its own echo in the more prolonged but hardly more exalted harmony of Milton's. He is the greatest discoverer, the most daring and inspired pioneer, in all our poetic literature. Before him there was neither genuine blank verse nor genuine tragedy in our language. After his arrival the way was prepared, the paths were made straight, for Shakespeare.

—Algernon Charles Swinburne, *The Age of Shakespeare* (London: Chatto & Windus, 1908): pp. 1, 6–7, 13–14.

U. M. ELLIS-FERMOR ON EDWARD II AS ENDEARING DEGENERATE

[Una Mary Ellis-Fermor was lecturer in English literature at Bedford College, University of London. She served as the General Editor of the New Arden Shakespeare and authored *Frontiers of Drama; Christopher Marlowe; Jacobean Drama: An Interpretation* and *Shakespeare the Dramatist.* Here she discusses Marlowe's methods of transforming *Edward II,* historically understood to be a "degenerate," into a moving and sympathetic character.]

This character, complex and subtle in its weakness, Marlowe has created from a very different record given him by his sources. The independence with which he treated chronology and the relations of the various characters in his play has often been noticed, but, great as is his freedom in that, it is over-shadowed by his reinterpretation of the character of the King. The historical Edward II revealed all the characteristics—most of them naturally unlovable—of a degenerate. He was a man of great physical strength and arrested mental development, fond of low company and of mechanical occupations, given to outbursts of physical violence and ungovernable passion, devoid of intelligence, but possessed of low cunning, perverted and unmanageable. Of this picture, Marlowe has taken part, just as he has followed in part the record of events, but he has transformed the details of the character and their bearing upon each other so that the man as a whole, although he frequently does what the historical Edward did, is a different figure. It is characteristic of Marlowe to convert all he touches to beauty: the dull impassivity of Edward in captivity becomes in his hands a gentle enduring of adversity; the notorious fondness for favourites, bluntly set down by the historian as perversion, becomes a not unbeautiful love-story against a dark background of storm and danger. Deliberately, and as if conscious of insight and sympathy which gave him the right so to interpret it, Marlowe reveals a complete, consistent and truly pathetic figure, the victim of the maladjustment of circumstances. His Edward is hardly strong enough to support a tragic fate, but he moves in pathos as his native atmosphere. He is too frail for the rôle which is thrust upon him, a rôle which he tries, nevertheless, to fulfil after his fashion, because while he lives, he is the keystone of the State and cannot be released from his position. The situation is one for which there is no remedy and in which the destruction of the victim is inevitable.

—U. M. Ellis-Fermor, *Christopher Marlowe* (London: Methuen & Co. Ltd., 1927): pp. 116–117.

Charles G. Masinton on Edward's Suffering

[Charles G. Masinton is Professor at the University of Kansas. He is the author of *Christopher Marlowe's Tragic Vision* and *J. P. Donleavy*. He has written articles on Vladimir Nabokov, Bernard Malamud, Thomas McGuane, and other contemporary fiction writers. Here he compares Edward with Marlowe's other protagonists, arguing that Edward uniquely demands compassion from the reader.]

Edward II, written in 1591 or 1592, marks a new stage in the development of Marlowe's dramaturgy. In stark contrast to the *Tamburlaine* plays and *The Jew of Malta*, whose protagonists represent abstract ideas more than they do real human beings, *Edward II* is a drama of character concentrating on the abnormal psychological states of its central figure. For all the excitement that we feel as we read Part I of *Tamburlaine* or see it performed, we are aware of the great emotional distance that separates us from the powerful yet sometimes inhuman Scythian. Tamburlaine is not a fully developed dramatic character; he is a symbol of mankind's urge to enjoy superhuman power. We are astonished by his brave exploits and his terri-fying ambitions, but our final reaction to him is less likely to be emotional than intellectual. We recognize that Tamburlaine is emblematic, that he represents a universal human attribute, but we do not sympathize with him.

With the figure of Edward our response is different. The proud but weak King, though at first an unattractive character, finally gains our sympathy because he is a severely flawed individual whose intense suffering demands our compassion. Edward becomes fully human (and wins back some of the dignity he care-lessly loses early in the play) only through experiencing great misery and gradually realizing the value of his lost kingship. Despite his cruelty to Isabella and his self-indulgent antics with Gaveston, it is his agony that makes the greatest impact on us. Charles Lamb has said that "the death-scene of Marlowe's king moves pity and terror beyond any scene ancient or modern with which I am acquainted." The violence and humiliation forced on the King build up during the play, until at the end a perfect crescendo of suffering is reached.

—Charles G. Masinton, *Christopher Marlowe's Tragic Vision: A Study in Damnation* (Athens, Ohio: Ohio University Press, 1972) pp. 86–87.

IRVING RIBNER ON THE EVOLUTION OF CHARACTER THROUGHOUT THE PLAY

[Irving Ribner (d.1972) served on the faculty at Tulane University and later was Professor of English at State University of New York at Stony Brook. He published a com-prehensive study of English history plays as well as a book on Jacobean tragedy. In this excerpt, Ribner discusses Isabella, Mortimer, and Edward II, contrasting them with characters from Marlowe's other works and arguing that Edward II depicts the evolution of character with unprece-dented depth and subtlety.]

. . . In Marlowe's *Edward II* we have the beginning of a type of histor-ical tragedy not based upon the Senecan formula, although the play displays a horror more moving than the Senecan clichés ever could, because it is more realistic. We have in *Edward II*, perhaps for the first time in Elizabethan drama, a tragedy of character in which a potentially good man comes to destruction because of inherent weaknesses which make him incapable of coping with a crisis which he himself has helped to create. And in his downfall he carries with him the sympathies of the audience. Like the traditional tragic hero he is a king, and his downfall is thus intimately involved with the life of the state, but in this instance Marlowe gives us a king drawn from the English chronicles, and in effecting his tragedy he accomplishes also the purposes of the Elizabethan historian. He interprets an earlier political situation which was of particular interest to Elizabethans, as we can tell from the many treatments of it in prose and verse, for it mirrored the type of civil war which they most dreaded. In *Edward II* tragedy and history are perfectly combined. Edward's sins are sins of government; the crisis he faces is a political one, and his disaster is ruin to his kingdom in the form of civil war. ⟨. . .⟩

As Edward falls, young Mortimer rises in his place, only to fall himself as the new King Edward III assumes his position. Edward and Mortimer are fashioned by Marlowe as protagonist and antagonist, two parallel characters, each serving as foil to the other. All of Edward's weaknesses are mirrored in Mortimer's strength; what private virtue Edward may have is set off by Mortimer's total lack of it. Those elements which cause Edward to fall cause Mortimer to rise. This use of two contrasting and complementary characters in tragedy Shakespeare was to learn from Marlowe in his *Richard II*, and he was to continue to use it in some of the greatest of his later plays.

We have already indicated that in his *Tamburlaine*, written some four or five years earlier, Marlowe had expressed a philosophy of history which was largely classical in origin. Marlowe, however, appears to have undergone some development between the two plays. The classical substantialism of *Tamburlaine*, with its resulting fixity of character, is now gone, and we find instead characters who change and develop under the pressure of events. This is as true of Mortimer and Isabella as it is of Edward; the adultress and the scheming traitor of the final scenes are hardly recognizable for the long suffering wife and the courageous patriot of the play's beginning. Edward changes and develops under the pressure of disaster, and his brother, Edmund, serves as a kind of chorus to guide the shifting sympathies of the audience. The tragedy of Edward would have been impossible within the substantialist framework of *Tamburlaine,* and only by abandoning it was Marlowe able to attain the stature of tragedy. We may attribute this change in large part to Marlowe's evident growth both in human understanding and in dramatic skill.

—Irving Ribner, *"Edward II* as a Historical Tragedy" (1957). In *Marlowe: Tamburlaine the Great, Edward the Second and The Jew of Malta,* ed. John Russell Brown (London: The Macmillan Press, 1982) pp. 140–142.

Works by
Christopher Marlowe

Tamburlaine the Great. 1592.

The Massacre at Paris. 1592.

Dido, Queen of Carthage. 1594.

Edward the Second. 1594.

Translation of *Ovid's Elegies.* 1596.

Hero and Leander. 1598.

Translation of *Lucan's First Book.* 1600.

Doctor Faustus ('A Text'). 1604.

Doctor Faustus ('B Text'). 1616.

The Jew of Malta. 1633.

Works about
Christopher Marlowe

Barber, C. L. *Creating Elizabethan Tragedy.* Chicago; London: The University of Chicago Press, 1988.

Bloom, Harold, ed., *Christopher Marlowe.* New York: Chelsea House Publishers, 1986.

————, ed., *Christopher Marlowe's Dr. Faustus.* New York: Chelsea House Publishers, 1988.

Boas, F. S. *Christopher Marlowe, A Biographical and Critical Study.* Oxford: The Clarendon Press, 1940.

Bradbrook, M. C. "A Discussion of *Tamburlaine.*" In *Critics on Marlowe,* ed. Judith O'Neill. London: George Allen and Unwin, 1969.

Bradley, A. C. "Christopher Marlowe." In *The English Poets: Selections,* ed. T. H. Ward. New York: Macmillan, 1880.

Cole, Douglas. *Christopher Marlowe and the Renaissance of Tragedy.* Westport, CT: Greenwood Press, 1995.

————. *Suffering and Evil in the Plays of Christopher Marlowe.* Princeton, N.J.: Princeton University Press, 1962.

Ellis-Fermor, Una Mary, ed., *Tamburlaine, the Great.* New York: Gordian Press, 1966.

Ellis-Fermor, Una Mary. *Christopher Marlowe.* Hamden, CT: Archon Books, 1967.

Empson, W. *Faustus and the Censor: the English Faust-book and Marlowe's 'Doctor Faustus.'* New York: Basil Blackwell, 1987.

English Institute. *Two Renaissance Mythmakers, Christopher Marlowe and Ben Jonson.* Edited, with a foreword, by Alvin Kernan. Baltimore: Johns Hopkins University Press, c1977.

Friedenreich, Kenneth, Roma Gill, and Constance B. Kuriyama, eds. *A Poet and a Filthy Play-Maker: New Essays on Christopher Marlowe.* New York: AMS Press, 1988.

Gardner, Helen "The Second Part of *Tamburlaine the Great.*" In *Critics on Marlowe,* ed. Judith O'Neill. London: George Allen and Unwin, 1969.

Giamatti, A. Bartlett. "The Arts of Illusion" in *Christopher Marlowe*. New York: Chelsea House, 1986.

Godshalk, W. L. *The Marlovian World Picture*. The Hague: Mouton, 1974.

Hope, A. D. "'Tamburlaine': The Argument of Arms" in *Christopher Marlowe*. New York: Chelsea House, 1986.

————. *The Cave and the Spring: Essays on Poetry*. Adelaide, Rigby; San Francisco: Tri-Ocean Books, 1965.

Knight, G. Wilson. *The Golden Labyrinth*. London: Phoenix House Ltd., 1962.

Kocher, P. H. *Christopher Marlowe: A Study of His Thoughts, Learning and Character*. New York: Russell & Russell, 1962.

Kuriyama, Constance Brown. *Hammer or Anvil: Psychological Patterns in Christopher Marlowe's Plays*. New Brunswick, N.J.: Rutgers University Press, c. 1980.

Leech, Clifford. Marlowe. *A Collection of Critical Essays*. New Jersey: Prentice Hall, 1964.

————. *Christopher Marlowe: Poet for the Stage*, ed. Anne Lancashire. New York: AMS Press, c. 1986.

Levin, Harry. *The Overreacher; A Study of Christopher Marlowe*. London: Faber & Faber, 1954.

MacLure, Millar. *Marlowe: The Critical Heritage, 1588–1896*. London; Boston: Routledge & K. Paul, 1979.

Masinton, Charles G. *Christopher Marlowe's Tragic Vision*. Athens, Ohio: Ohio University Press, 1972.

Nuttall, A. D. *The Alternative Trinity: Gnostic Heresy in Marlowe, Milton, and Blake*. Oxford; New York: Clarendon Press, 1998.

Palmer, D. J. "Marlowe's Naturalism" in *Mermaid Critical Commentaries: Christopher Marlowe*, ed. Brian Norris. New York: Hill and Wang, 1968.

Proser, Matthew N. "*Tamburlaine I* and the Art of Destruction" in *The Gift of Fire: Aggression and the Plays of Christopher Marlowe*. New York: Peter Lang, 1995.

Ribner, Irving. "*Edward II* as a Historical Tragedy" (1957). In *Marlowe: Tamburlaine the Great, Edward the Second and The Jew of Malta*, ed. John Russell Brown. London: The Macmillan Press, 1982.

―――. *The English History Play in the Age of Shakespeare.* New York: Barnes & Noble, 1965.

Rossiter, A. P. *English Drama from Early Times to the Elizabethans.* London; New York: Hutchinson's University Library,1959.

Sanders, Wilbur. *The Dramatist and the Received Idea; Studies in the Plays of Marlowe & Shakespeare.* London: Cambridge University Press, 1968.

Swinburne, Algernon Charles. *The Age of Shakespeare.* London: Chatto and Windus, 1908.

Tydeman, William. *Christopher Marlowe: A Guide Through the Critical Maze.* Bristol: Bristol Classical Press, 1989.

Walker, A. R. and Glover, Arnold, eds., *The Collected Works of William Hazlitt.* London: J. M. Dent & Co., 1902.

Index of
Themes and Ideas

DR. FAUSTUS, 71–80; Belzebub in, 76; characters in, 75–76; critical views on, 49, 63, 77–88, 99; Evil Angel in, 71, 75, 79; Faustus in, 10, 63, 71–74, 75, 77–83, 84–85, 86, 87–88; Faustus' thirst for knowledge in, 77–78; Good Angel in, 71, 75, 87; and *The Jew of Malta,* 63; Lucifer in, 72, 73, 76, 79; Mephastophiles in, 72–73, 74, 75–76, 78–81; Old Man in, 74, 76; plot summary of, 71–74; predestination in, 86–88; relationship of Mephastophiles and Faustus in, 78–80; Renaissance idealism *vs.* Christian theology in, 80–82; subplot in, 82–83; tragic effect in, 84–85; Valdes and Cornelius in, 71, 75; Wagner in, 71, 72, 74, 75, 83

EDWARD II, 89–104; Baldock in, 69, 91, 96; Bishop of Coventry in, 69, 89; black comedy in, 68–69; characters in, 94–96; critical views on, 10, 68–69, 79, 82, 97–104; Lady Margaret De Clare in, 95; Edmund in, 92, 94, 104; Edward II as degenerate in, 100–101; Edward II in, 10, 68, 69, 79, 82, 89–90, 91–92, 93, 94, 97–98, 99, 100–102, 103, 104; Edward II's death in, 68, 92, 97–98, 99, 102; Edward II's suffering in, 101–2; Prince Edward in, 92, 93, 94; evolution of character in, 102–4; Piers Gaveston in, 69, 89, 90, 91, 98, 102; Gurner and Matrevis in, 92, 96; Isabella in, 89–90, 91, 92, 93, 94, 102, 103; and *The Jew of Malta,* 102; Kent in, 90, 91, 92; Lightborn in, 92, 96, 97; Mortimer Junior in, 68, 89, 90, 91, 92, 93, 95, 103–4; Mortimer Senior in, 89, 90, 94; Earl of Arundel in, 91, 95; Earl of Lancaster in, 95; Earl of Leicester and Bishop of Winchester in, 91, 92, 95; Earl of Pembroke in, 91, 95; plot summary of, 89–93; Spencer Junior in, 91, 96; Spencer Senior in, 95–96; and *Tamburlaine,* 102, 103–4; Warwick in, 69, 91, 95; weaknesses of, 97

JEW OF MALTA, THE, 54–70; Abigail in, 55–56, 59, 66, 69; Ballamira in, 56, 57, 60, 62, 69; Barabas as hero-villain in, 63–64; Barabas as symbol of evil in, 64–66; Barabas in, 10, 13–14, 54–55, 56, 57, 58, 61–67, 68, 69, 79, 81–82, 102; Barabas' suffering in, 61; Friar Bernardine in, 56, 60, 66; black comedy in, 68–70; Callapine in, 59; characters in, 58–60; critical views on, 10, 13–14, 27, 61–70, 79, 81–82, 99; Martin Del Bosco in, 55, 60; and *Dr. Faustus,* 63; and *Edward II,* 102; Ferneze in, 54, 55, 57, 58, 61, 66–68, 69, 70; Ferneze's seizure of Barabas' wealth in, 54, 66–68; Ithamore in, 13–14, 55, 56, 57, 59, 65, 69; Katherine in, 55, 59; Don Lodowick in, 55, 56, 59, 66; Machevill in, 54, 58; Machiavellian spirit in, 54, 55, 58, 61–62, 64, 65, 68; Don Mathias